CULTURES OF THE WORLD
Norway

Cavendish
Square

New York

Published in 2017 by Cavendish Square Publishing, LLC
243 5th Avenue, Suite 136 New York, NY 10016
Copyright © 2017 by Cavendish Square Publishing, LLC

Third Edition

This publication represents the opinions and views of the author based on his or her personal experience, knowledge, and research. The information in this book serves as a general guide only. The author and publisher have used their best efforts in preparing this book and disclaim liability rising directly or indirectly from the use and application of this book.
CPSIA Compliance Information: Batch #CS16CSQ
All websites were available and accurate when this book was sent to press.

Cataloging-in-Publication Data

Names: Kagda, Sakina.
Title: Norway / Sakina Kagda, Barbara Cooke, and Debbie Nevins, third edition.
Description: New York : Cavendish Square, 2017. | Series: Cultures of the world | Includes index.
Identifiers: ISBN 9781502618481 (library bound) | ISBN 9781502618498 (ebook)
Subjects: LCSH: Norway--Juvenile literature.
Classification: LCC DL409.K34 2017 | DDC 948.1--dc23

Writers: Sakina Kagda, Barbara Cooke; Debbie Nevins, third edition
Editorial Director, third edition: David McNamara
Editor, third edition: Debbie Nevins
Art Director, third edition: Jeffrey Talbot
Designer, third edition: Jessica Nevins
Production Assistant, third edition: Karol Szymczuk
Cover Picture Researcher: Jeffrey Talbot
Picture Researcher, third edition: Jessica Nevins

PICTURE CREDITS

The photographs in this book are used with the permission of: LOOK Die Bildagentur der Fotografen GmbH/Alamy, cover; Mostovyi Sergii Igorevich, 1; Anibal Trejo/Shutterstock.com, 3; Grisha Bruev/Shutterstock.com, 5; Lijuan Guo/Shutterstock.com, 6; ODD ANDERSEN/AFP/Getty Images, 7; JONATHAN NACKSTRAND/AFP/Getty Images, 8; mihaiulia/Shutterstock.com, 10; Thorsten Link/Shutterstock.com, 13; Anna Jedynak/ Shutterstock.com, 14; Anibal Trejo/Shutterstock.com, 16; Tsuguliev/Shutterstock.com, 18; BMJ/Shutterstock.com, 20; Lasse Hendriks/Shutterstock. com, 21; Vladimirs1984/Shutterstock.com, 22; Ravelios/Shutterstock.com, 24; Andreas Gradin/Shutterstock.com, 26; Fine Art Images/Heritage Images/ Getty Images, 28; Scandphoto/Shutterstock.com, 33; Anna Jedynak/Shutterstock.com, 36; Jørgen Gomnæs, the Royal Court via Getty Images, 39; Francis Apesteguy/Getty Images, 41; Christian Fredrik Wesenberg (Flickr)/File:Erna Solberg, Wesenberg, 2011 (2).jpg/Wikimedia Commons, 42; OLIVIER MORIN/AFP/Getty Images, 43; National Library of Norway/File:Portrett av Anna Rogstad (8055961979).jpg/Wikimedia Commons, 44; John Lamparski/Getty Images, 45; HEIKO JUNGE/AFP/Getty Images, 46; Eder/Shutterstock.com, 48; V. Belov/Shutterstock.com, 50; Juan Samoral Franco/Shutterstock.com, 52; Nikitina Oksana/Shutterstock.com, 53; Christian Wilkinson/Shutterstock.com, 54; Adam Przezak/Shutterstock.com, 56; Morten Falch Sortland/Moment Open/Getty Images, 59; Tupungato/Shutterstock.com, 61; carballo/Shutterstock.com, 64; Clara/Shutterstock.com, 66; Vlada Photo/Shutterstock.com, 67; Underwood & Underwood/Alinari Archives, Florence/Alinari via Getty Images, 69; Fishman/ullstein bild via Getty Images, 71; Berzina/Shutterstock.com, 72; Marzolino/Shutterstock.com, 75; Grisha Bruev/Shutterstock.com, 80; Photo12/UIG via Getty Images, 83; Medioimages/Photodisc/Getty Images, 84; Renata Sedmakova/Shutterstock.com, 86; Ingunn B. Haslekås/Moment Mobile/Getty Images, 88; Røed/File:Målformer i Norge.svg/Wikimedia Commons, 92; A.Sandberg/Shutterstock.com, 92; VICTOR TORRES/Shutterstock.com, 94; Universal History Archive/UIG via Getty Images, 97; Imagno/Getty Images, 99; Nicku/Shutterstock.com, 101; ullstein bild/ullstein bild via Getty Images, 101; Claudia Carlsen/Shutterstock.com, 103; V. Belov/Shutterstock.com, 104; my nordic/Shutterstock.com, 106; Quinn Rooney/Getty Images, 109; Laila R/Shutterstock.com, 110; Tony Duffy/Allsport/Getty Images, 111; DeAgostini/Getty Images, 112; Andrea Izzotti/Shutterstock.com, 113; ullstein bild/ ullstein bild via Getty Images, 114; Nanisimova/Shutterstock.com, 116; Albert H. Teich/Shutterstock.com, 119; TasfotoNL/Shutterstock.com, 120; Nikolaidi/Shutterstock.com, 122; from my point of view/Shutterstock.com, 124; Tupungato/Shutterstock.com, 125; Amy Kerkemeyer/Shutterstock. com, 126; Fishman/ullstein bild via Getty Images, 127; Jeffrey B. Banke/Shutterstock.com, 129; Fanfo/Shutterstock.com, 130; Tyler Nevins, 131.

PRECEDING PAGE

Young hikers sit in front of an old traditional wooden house in Tyin, Norway.

Printed in the United States of America

CONTENTS

NORWAY TODAY

I **N MORE WAYS THAN ONE, NORWAY IS SITTING ON TOP OF THE** world. For one thing, it is one of the northernmost countries on Earth. About half of it sits above the Arctic Circle, and the town of Longyearbyen, on Norway's Svalbard archipelago, is the world's northernmost town.

In fact, the name "Norway" means "north way." The etymology, or word history, of the name is quite interesting. The country was originally called norðrvegr in Old Norse (Nordweg in Old English), which means "the northern way" or "the way north." Today, the people who live in Norway call their country Noreg or Norge. The syllable *nor*, also found in the words "Nordic" and "Norse," means "north." (In English, the adjective "Norwegian" retains the syllable *weg* from the Old English name—which is why Norwegians aren't called Norwayans.)

Being at the top of the world means Norway has twenty-four hours of sunshine in the summertime—in the northern part of the country, that is. (Of course in the wintertime, the opposite is true.) The midnight sun, as it's called, is a wondrous sight for those who live at the top of the world. The same can be said for the northern lights, or aurora borealis, the celestial lightshow that can usually be seen only in

A display of the northern lights appears over Ersfjorden, in Tromso, Norway.

the far north. The world's first northern lights observatory was built in Alta, the largest town in Finnmark, Norway, at the end of the nineteenth century, thereby giving Alta the nickname "The Town of the Northern Lights." Norwegian travel companies schedule numerous northern lights-themed cruises and tours. In 2013, northern lights tourism brought some 200 million kroner ($24 million) into the country.

Norway is on top of the world in other ways, too. It's consistently ranked the most livable country in the world, according to the United Nations (UN) Human Development Index. Norway regularly shares this distinction with its neighboring Scandinavian countries, Sweden, Finland, and Denmark, which also rank at the top of quality-of-life indexes.

It helps that Norway is a wealthy nation. Its healthy economy, based on the abundant oil discovered off its northern coast several decades ago, certainly adds bonus points to its livability. Another reason Norway ranks so high is that it's a very egalitarian society. Norwegians care deeply about issues such as human rights, civil rights, and gender equality. Compared to many other nations, Norway has some of the lowest income inequality in the world—meaning the distribution of wealth is more evenly balanced than in most other countries. It also has comparatively low unemployment, poverty, and crime rates.

In terms of crime, Norway is so safe, relatively speaking, that police officers are usually unarmed. In times of heightened alerts, such as in the aftermath of the Brussels terror attacks in March 2016, Norwegian police may be ordered to carry weapons, but ordinarily, their arms are kept locked within police vehicles. Great Britain, Ireland, Iceland, and New Zealand are the other countries where this is the case. In 2015, Norway's police fired their guns only twice, and no one was hurt. In the twelve years prior to that, the police killed only two people. Norway also has a low prison rate, with less than four thousand of its five million citizens in jail—and it has a low rate of recidivism, or repeated criminal behavior, among prisoners as well. At a time when US prisons are overcrowded and police shootings of unarmed individuals is a concern, Norway's tradition of unarmed police is noteworthy.

On July 26, 2011, a boy places flowers at a makeshift memorial in Oslo for the victims of the July 22 attacks.

All the more reason, perhaps, why Norway—along with the rest of the world—was especially shocked by the mass killings at a summer camp on the small island of Utøya in July 2011. The lone gunman, dressed as a policeman himself, killed seventy-seven people in two separate attacks in one day. He killed eight people in Oslo before ferrying out to the youth camp. His first victim on the island was an unarmed police officer.

After the massacre, law enforcement officials were criticized for their allegedly inept response. It took the police some ninety minutes to get to the island, far more time than it should have. The incident illustrates the new challenges that Norway faces in the twenty-first century. Immigration is one of the greatest of those challenges. The gunman, Anders Behring Breivik, said his rampage was meant to fight multiculturalism, and particularly the increasing Muslim population. The young people at the camp were Norwegians, but some were immigrants. In recent years, Norway has seen a large uptick in immigrants and asylum seekers, due in part to the civil war in Syria. In 2015 alone, more than thirty thousand refugees arrived in Norway—mainly from Syria, Iraq, and Afghanistan. That number was up from about 11,500 the year before. In 2015, immigrants made up 15.6 percent of Norway's population. What was once a relatively white, Christian country is rapidly changing, and Norway is trying hard to adapt with grace and positivity. The nation prides itself on inclusion, tolerance, and openness; however, the large influx of immigrants puts Norway's cherished values to the test. Some of the newcomers bring traditions and attitudes with them that clash with Norwegian ways. To help people adjust to their new home,

People rest at the arrival center for refugees near the town of Kirkenes in northern Norway, which is close to the Russian border, in 2015. That border has been an increasingly popular route for migrants trying to get to Norway.

Norway is trying to educate those newcomers in European culture and social mores.

Although Norway has, so far, avoided the full force of the mass refugee exodus that has affected Greece and other Mediterranean countries in recent years, the rise in immigrants has been a challenge for Norwegian politicians. As welcoming as it wants to be, Norway cannot accept all of the desperate people who cross its borders. In April 2016, Norwegian authorities unveiled a new plan to pay asylum seekers to leave the country voluntarily, saying the expense would save the government money over the cost of supporting large numbers of people in the immigration centers.

Despite these challenges, Norway is doing very well indeed. Some observers, however, wonder if the country can keep the good times rolling. What will happen when the oil runs out? Can Norway diversify its economic base before that happens? Can the welfare state survive as it is now, or will a depleted economy chip away at the benefits? Even if a post-oil scenario is a long way off, Norway's leaders are contemplating it now.

Meanwhile, though, there are some assets Norway can rely on. Its magnificent mountains and fjords attracted more than five million tourists in 2013. Its Viking heritage fascinates people at home and abroad. In spring 2016, the Draken Harald Hårfagre ("Dragon Harald Fairhair"), a 115-foot (35-meter), replica Viking longship set out from Norway to relive the almost mythological first Viking transatlantic crossing and discovery of the New World more than one thousand years ago. If the Vikings could venture forth to an unknown world, surely today's Norway is more than ready to tackle its modern challenges.

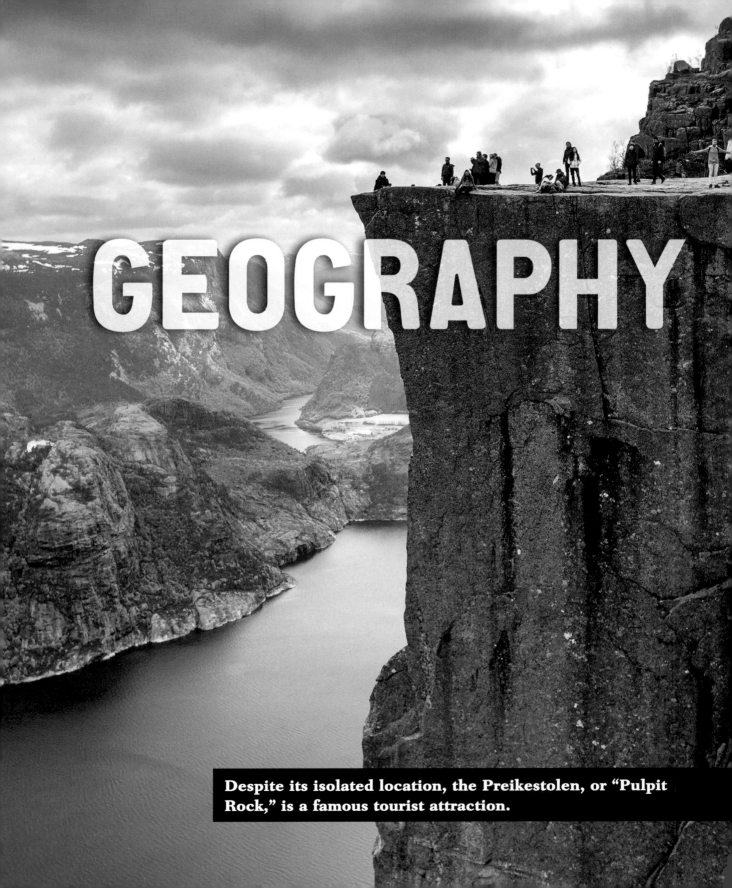

GEOGRAPHY

Despite its isolated location, the Preikestolen, or "Pulpit Rock," is a famous tourist attraction.

1

S HAPED LIKE A LONG-HANDLED spoon, or ladle, Norway stretches along the western and northern coasts of the Scandinavian Peninsula at the top of the European continent. It is a spoon with a very jagged edge, however—Norway has one of the longest and most rugged coastlines in the world. The coast rises up steeply from the North Sea and the North Atlantic Ocean, and is characterized by deeply indented inlets and fifty thousand islands, all carved out by glaciers about ten thousand years ago. With all its zigs and zags, the coastline measures some 15,626 miles (25,148 kilometers). The mainland coast, without all its craggy indentations, stretches about 1,647 miles (2,650 km).

In area, though certainly not in shape, Norway is about the size of New Mexico. Nearly two-thirds of the mainland is mountainous, and its 160,000 lakes are also a testament to the tremendous masses of ice, earth, and rock that carved out the country's topography during the time of the ancient glaciers.

Rising almost 2,000 feet (604 meters) above the Lysefjord, a fjord in southwestern Norway, Pulpit Rock is a flat-topped cliff with a smooth pinnacle measuring about 82 feet by 82 feet (25 m by 25 m). The unusual rock is difficult to access, but that hasn't prevented some 200,000 people from visiting it each year. Norwegian authorities have opted not to install fencing because it would detract from the site's natural beauty. Despite the danger, there have been very few fatalities over the years.

MOUNTAINS

Norway is one of the most mountainous countries in Europe. The Scandinavian Mountains extend almost the entire length of the country. Glaciers shaped the peaks into such odd forms that they have provoked images of trolls and supernatural spirits. The mountains in the South, which contain the highest peaks in Europe north of the Alps, are called Jotunheimen, or "Realm of the Giants."

A few mountains are so steep that no one has ever attempted to scale them. Others have been attempted only in recent years. The 2,000-foot (610 m) Reka in northern Norway has never been climbed. The Troll Wall in Romsdal (western Norway) was first climbed in 1967. Many consider it the most demanding climb in Europe. The retreating glaciers cut some mountains down into *vidder* (VI-der), or mountain plateaus; others were ground down by the weight of the ice sheet, 1.25 miles (2 km) thick, into flat plateaus called *fjell* (fyehl). The most impressive legacy of the glacial erosion in the uplands are the fjords (fyords) of western Norway. These are very deep and narrow inlets of the sea between steep cliffs. The fjords of Norway are sometimes deeper even than the North Sea, although they are often shallower near the coast, where the ice sheet is thinner.

REGIONS

The Norwegians have divided their country into five main regions according to geography and dialects. Vestlandet (West Country), Østlandet (East Country), Sørlandet (South Country), and Trøndelag (Mid-Norway) make up South Norway. Nord-Norge (North Norway) makes up the rest.

In southern Norway, Sørlandet, the smallest region, is located at the southernmost point. The other three main regions of the south are defined by wide mountain barriers. From the southernmost point, a swelling complex of mountain ranges, collectively called Langfjellene, or Long Mountains, runs northward to divide Østlandet from Vestlandet. An eastward sweep of mountains separates the northern edge of Østlandet from Trøndelag. Where the southern half of Norway ends, northern Norway, or Nord-Norge, begins.

FJORDS

In total, there are about 1,190 fjords in Norway and the Svalbard Islands.

The Sognefjord is the largest and deepest fjord in Norway, and the second-largest in the world. It stretches 127 miles (205 km) inland from the ocean to the small village of Skjolden in the municipality of Luster. The fjord reaches a maximum depth of 4,291 ft (1,308 m) below sea level, and the greatest depths are found in the inland parts of the fjord. Cliffs surrounding the fjord rise almost sheer from the water to heights of 3,300 ft (1,000 m) and more.

Nærøyfjord, a branch of the Sognefjord particularly noted for its unspoiled nature and dramatic scenery, and only 980 ft (300 m) across at its narrowest point. The Nærøyfjord is a UNESCO World Heritage Site.

VESTLANDET With well-kept villages and coastal towns nestled against a backdrop of majestic mountains, the West Country represents the Norway best known to the rest of the world—the picturesque Norway. The ancestors of many Norwegian American immigrants left this area in the nineteenth century. This narrow coastal zone reaches into the Atlantic Ocean and has many islands and steep-walled narrow fjords cutting deep into the interior mountain region. The major exception is the Jæren plain, south of the city of Stavanger, which has the highest agricultural yields in Norway due to its rich soils, very mild winters, long growing season, and abundant rainfall.

SØRLANDET Centered around the city of Kristiansand, this southern area has an idyllic coastline that has become Norway's foremost summer vacation area. The land is hilly, but the agricultural season is slightly longer than

The Oslo skyline is seen from the waters of the Oslofjord, an inlet that leads to the Skagerrak Strait and out to the North Sea.

in Oslo, Norway's capital. The interior of Sørlandet, with its narrow valleys running up into the beginnings of Langfjellene, is very sparsely populated. The people of the scattered settlements there depend on dairy farming, sheep raising, and forestry.

ØSTLANDET   The East Country boasts more than half of Norway's population, who live mainly in and around the metropolis of Oslo and in the region around Oslofjord. Although this area is mostly urban and industrial, there is also agriculture, which is found mainly in the lowlands extending eastward and southward toward the Swedish border. The lowlands are intensively cultivated due to favorable conditions such as sufficient rain, the highest summer temperatures in Norway, and rich soil. The largest forests in Norway are found between the Swedish border and the Glåma River, east of Oslo. The coastline facing Denmark across the Skagerrak passage, stretching from Oslofjord to the southern tip of Norway, is densely populated and crowded with small towns, villages, and farms.

About half of Østlandet is forested. The region has a little more than half of Norway's total forest resources and a similar share of the country's total area of fully cultivated land. Østlandet also accounts for more than half of the nation's total production value and trade in the mining and manufacturing industries. These large shares of the national wealth, combined with the concentration of economic activity around Oslofjord, secure for Østlandet the highest average household income in Norway.

TRØNDELAG Mid-Norway, also known as the Trøndelag region, is centered around the long Trondheimfjord. Trondheim, the region's major city, is the third largest in Norway. Trøndelag has less industrial development than Østlandet and Vestlandet because there are few suitable sites for power stations. On the eastern shore of the fjord is a small agricultural area.

NORD-NORGE Mountains with jagged peaks and ridges fill most of this region, even the many islands. A long string of large islands jutting into the Atlantic west of Vestfjorden form the Lofoten archipelago. Numerous fjords scissor into this narrow strip of Norway's northern tail. Northern Norway has one of the most irregular coastlines in the world, even more irregular than in the southwest. Nord-Norge has a rugged frontier quality about it, fitting for life in the far north.

Nord-Norge has been called the "the weather kitchen of Europe." Rain, clouds, mist, and fog are characteristic of much of the Norwegian coast, but gales and squalls add a special quality to the north, which has recorded some of the highest wind speeds in the world. Norway's first meteorological station was established there in 1866. As is often said in Nord-Norge, there is a lot of weather to watch.

CLIMATE

Without the warm waters of the Gulf Stream, which keep the fjords from freezing, Norway's coastal areas would not enjoy such a temperate and mild climate year round. Even beyond the North Cape, which is farther north than both Siberia and the continent of North America, there are many green forests, and, on sunny days, the beaches are strewn with sunbathers.

Average temperatures for the southern part of Norway near Oslo and Bergen range from freezing in winter to 61 degrees Farenheit (16 degrees

The duration of daylight and night varies from one place to another due to the tilt of the earth's axis and the season of the year. At the equator there is hardly any noticeable difference between the number of hours of daylight and darkness, or between summer and winter. The farther north or south one goes, however, the greater the variation. Located as far north as it is, Norway experiences great variations in seasons and in hours of daylight and night.

In the northern half of Norway, the sun does not set all summer. The area from the Arctic Circle to the North Cape is called the Land of the Midnight Sun, and attracts thousands of tourists. The length of time the sun stays above the horizon declines as one goes south, but the sun never sets on Midsummer's Day (June 23) in all places north of the Arctic Circle.

Even south of the Arctic Circle, summer nights are so bright that people can read their newspapers by natural light in the middle of the night. It is not unusual for Norwegians to take a walk or visit friends at 2 a.m. Norwegians say they have two days for every summer day: one for work and one for hverdagslivet (vehr-DAHGS-leev-uht) or daily life.

To make up for all that daylight during summer, those who live north of the Arctic Circle will not see the sun for weeks in winter, although there usually is some daylight around midday.

Celsius) in summer. In northern Norway, the average winter temperature is 23°F (-5°C), and the average summer temperature is about 50°F (10°C), although temperatures have been known to reach as high as 77 to 86°F (25—30°C).

Norway lies directly in the path of the North Atlantic cyclones, which bring strong winds and frequent changes in weather. Western Norway experiences comparatively cool summers, mild winters, and a substantial amount of rain. Eastern Norway, sheltered by the mountains in the center of the country, experiences warm summers, cold winters, and very little rain.

NEW TERRITORIES

In the late nineteenth century, Fridtjof Nansen's polar expedition came within 272 miles (438 km) of the North Pole. Less than two decades later, Roald Amundsen's expedition was the first to reach the South Pole. Norwegian exploration in polar regions brought new territories under Norway's sovereignty: Svalbard in 1925, Bouvet Island in 1928, Jan Mayen Island in 1929, Peter I Island in 1931, and Dronning Maud Land in 1939.

SVALBARD This archipelago located in the Arctic, 352 miles (567 km) from the northernmost point of mainland Norway, consists of four large islands and a number of small ones covering an area of 38,5572 square miles (998,627 square kilometers). The largest of the islands, Spitsbergen, accounts for more than half of the archipelago's total land area. The landscape is characterized by steep mountains and deep fjords, and vast areas are covered by glaciers. Coal mining constitutes the main economic activity. Svalbard's population of around 2,700 people is concentrated at Longyearbyen, Ny-Ålesund, Barentsburg, and Pyramiden.

ANTARCTIC ISLANDS Norway's three territories in the Antarctic are Bouvet Island, Peter I Island, and Dronning Maud Land. Norway was one of twelve countries that signed the Antarctic Treaty in 1959. In 1991 these countries agreed to maintain the Antarctic as a nature reserve devoted to peace, research, and environmental cooperation. Mineral extraction activity in the area is prohibited for fifty years from the 1991 treaty.

When the sun reappears in late January, after two months of continous darkness, children in Tromsø, in northern Norway, get the day off from school to watch its arrival. They have to be on the alert to greet the sun, as it is above the horizon for only four minutes on that day.

THE LOFOTEN ARCHIPELAGO

This summertime aerial view shows the village of Reine on the very tip of the Lofoten Islands.

The mountains on various Lofoten islands are sometimes referred to as the Lofoten Wall, perhaps because its islands form a barrier between the northwestern coast of Norway and the Atlantic Ocean. The total area of the Lofoten islands is 475 square miles (1,230 sq km), and the principal islands are Austvågøy, Vestvågøy, and Moskenesøy. The Lofoten islands are famous for their fisheries. Commercial anglers crowd the fishing villages on the islands during the cod season, from January to April. The Norwegian Fishing Village Museum and the Dried Fish Museum are both located at Lofoten.

MAJOR CITIES

Norway's three major cities are Oslo, the capital and home to about 530,000 people; Bergen, with a population of almost 240,000; and Trondheim, which ranks third with 157,000 people.

OSLO Norway's capital, situated at the head of the Oslofjord, is the country's main hub for communications, trade, education, research, industry, and transportation. It is also Norway's political and financial heart, and its center for international shipping. Oslo was founded by King Harald III around 1050, but only became the capital of Norway in the fourteenth century. Destroyed by fire in 1624 and rebuilt as Christiania, it was renamed Oslo in 1924.

BERGEN The natural center of Vestlandet, Bergen has a more international character than any other city in Norway. Since the Middle Ages, it was an active trading center of northern Europe. It was officially founded in 1070 by King Olav III, "The Peaceful" (ruled 1069—1093). Unlike Trondheim and Oslo, Bergen has no fertile land. It lies amid seven mountains facing the sea. Said to have been a starting point for many Viking seafaring expeditions, Bergen grew as a fishing and trading port.

Present-day Bergen is the second-largest city in Norway and is still the principal port on the west coast, with a considerable merchant fleet, several large shipyards, and one of Norway's six universities.

TRONDHEIM Trondheim, in Trøndelag, is Norway's historic capital. It was founded in 997 by Viking king Olav Tryggvason (ruled 995—1000). In the Middle Ages, Trondheim was an important commercial, administrative, and religious core. Norway's first abbey was built on an island outside the city, and Nidaros Cathedral, an important pilgrimage site, is also there.

Trondheim, Norway's technology capital, has been a research center since as early as 1760, when Norway's Royal Scientific Society founded a museum and research station in the city. Norway's first seat of learning is a school founded by the Nidaros Cathedral monks. In 1900 the technical school was transformed into a college, known today as the Norwegian Institute of Technology. SINTEF (The Foundation for Scientific and Industrial Research) at the Norwegian Institute of Technology is a state-funded research institute that concentrates on marine and information technology in Norway and abroad. The national Ship Research Institute is located there, as well as a biological research station with an aquarium.

OTHER CITIES Apart from being the oil capital of Norway, Stavanger in southwest Norway is the prime area for agricultural research. Tromsø, Norway's largest city north of the Arctic Circle, is home to the world's leading research organization for the Arctic phenomena.

FAUNA AND FLORA

Reindeer, wolverines, and other Arctic animals live throughout Norway, although in the south they are found only in mountain areas. Elk are found

A Norway lemming feeds on grass.

in the forests and red deer populate the west coast. Although common as recently as one hundred years ago, bear, wolf, wolverine, and lynx are found in only a few areas, mainly in the north. Foxes and otters are common, and badgers and beavers inhabit many areas. The abundance of beaver is an example of a successful protection program. Prior to 1940, the entire European stock of beaver was around five hundred or so, and those beavers were found largely in southern Norway. State protection increased their population to the extent that Norway was able to send beavers to Switzerland, Russia, and the Czech Republic.

A small rodent commonly found in areas of Norway is the lemming. People speak of a lemming year, when mountainous regions teem with thousands of these small animals, providing predators with a rich food source. The dazzlingly white snowy owl of the North Pole will fly thousands of miles to a good supply of lemmings. How it knows when lemmings are plentiful is one of nature's mysteries.

Nesting cliffs are filled with millions of kittiwakes, puffins, guillemots, auks, cormorants, and gulls. The sea eagle, classified as an endangered species about fifty years ago, is now thriving. Lakes and marshes are inhabited by cranes, whooper swans, grebes, geese, ducks, and other waders.

Along the coast there are large numbers of seals and whales. Most rivers have fish, notably trout and salmon. Large schools of salmon are found in at least 160 rivers, attracting anglers from all over the world.

Norway has about two thousand species of plants, but only a few, mainly mountain plants, are particular to Norway. Thick forests of spruce and pine thrive in the broad glacial valleys of eastern Norway and in the Trondheim region. In western Norway there are virtually no conifers. North of the Arctic

Circle there is little spruce, and pine grows mainly in the inland valleys. The pine, spruce, and other Norwegian conifers, such as juniper and yew, retain their needlelike leaves throughout the year. In winter the needles curl up to retain moisture.

Wild berries grow throughout Norway, including blueberries, cranberries, and cloudberries, a species that belongs to the rose family and is little known outside Scandinavia and the United Kingdom.

The climate is a prime factor in determining the distribution patterns of plant life in Norway. Along the west coast, where winter is mild and snowfalls rare, plants that cannot tolerate frost thrive, such as the star hyacinth and purple heather. Farther inland grow species that can withstand short periods of frost and snow in the winter: the foxglove and holly are typical plants. Around Oslo, the long, cold winter and dry, warm summer provide the right climate for species like the blue anemone and the aconite.

Cloudberries are sometimes called "highland gold" in Norway. They are not grown commercially and can only be attained by hand-picking in the wild.

INTERNET LINKS

www.lonelyplanet.com/norway
This travel site has many nice image galleries and maps.

www.visitnorway.com
This is another attractive travel site with excellent photos and maps.

HISTORY

The earliest inhabitants of Norway lived in shelters like this one.

2

EVER SINCE THE GLACIAL ICE receded, some ten thousand years ago, there have been humans living in Norway. The earliest evidence was found along the coast of Finnmark and north of Stadlandet in the west. Archaeologists believe these people lived between 9000 BCE and 8000 BCE, by which time most of the glacial ice had receded. These earliest inhabitants may have migrated from Finland and Russia around 10,000 BCE, when the interior was still covered with ice. Another theory is that they came considerably later from the south and traveled northward.

THE EARLIEST FARMERS

Before 3000 BCE, the inhabitants of Norway lived in tentlike shelters and coastal mountain caves. They hunted and fished. Between 3000 BCE and 1500 BCE, warlike Germanic tribes migrated to Norway. From them, the earlier inhabitants learned to attach handles to tools to make them more efficient. During this period eastern Norway was settled by other

> "If there is anyone who still wonders why this war is being fought, let him look to Norway. If there is anyone who has any delusions that this war could have been averted, let him look to Norway; and if there is anyone who doubts the democratic will to win, again I say, let him look to Norway"
> —US President Franklin D. Roosevelt, December 1942, praising Norway's resistance to Nazi German occupation during World War II

A replica of a Viking longship sails among the Lofoten Islands in Norway.

migrants—farmers who grew barley and kept cows and sheep. The hunter-fishers of the west coast were gradually replaced by these farmers, although hunting and fishing remained in use. This gave rise to permanent farming settlements, which were usually situated along the coast and near lakes.

Isolated from each other by mountains and fjords, the farming communities became independent small states with their own leaders. By the eighth century, thirty states existed in Norway. By the ninth century, the states were divided into districts, each with its own assembly, where grievances were settled in accordance with written laws.

THE VIKINGS

Perhaps the most famous Scandinavians are the Vikings. In the Viking Age (793—1066 CE), the Scandinavians set out over the oceans to conquer new territories and expand their markets. One theory behind this desire for conquest is that the rapid population growth that seems to have occurred

The origin of the word "Viking" has long been a mystery. Some scholars believe it means "creekmen," basing this on the Old Norse word vic, *meaning creek or inlet. Others insist it refers to a pirating center, the Vik, in the Oslofjord. Yet another theory is that the term originated from the Old English word* wic, *meaning "warrior."*

The Europeans whose lands were invaded by Vikings did not speculate much on the origin of the term and did not differentiate Swedish Vikings from Danish Vikings or Norwegian Vikings. They simply referred to them as "men from the north"—Norsemen or Northmen. A popular prayer in the ninth century was, "From the fury of the Northmen, deliver us, O Lord." The early Vikings themselves identified with their local districts, calling themselves "men of Hardanger" or "men of Vestfold." Only toward the end of the Viking Age did a concept of national identity begin to develop.

from 600 CE led to a shortage of land, prompting many to look overseas for their fortunes. The Vikings came from Norway, Sweden, and Denmark, and each had different routes of conquest and trade.

The Vikings were the only Western sailors in early medieval times who dared to sail beyond landmarks into uncharted waters. They discovered Svalbard, the Arctic islands northwest of Norway. Before 1000 CE, they had settled in all the habitable islands in the North Atlantic, including the Shetlands, the Orkneys, the Faeroe Islands, Iceland, and Greenland, which all remained under Norwegian influence for centuries. They also landed on the shores of North America some five hundred years before Christopher Columbus did, but their settlements there did not last.

VIOLENT VIKINGS The Vikings had a reputation of being pirates because of their warlike raids on other European communities. These characterized the first hundred years of the Viking Age. The earliest recorded raid of the Norwegian Vikings was in 793. Landing quickly and unexpectedly on the island of Lindisfarne, off the northeast coast of England, a small party of raiders looted the monastery, set it on fire, slaughtered many monks, and took others captive. They then sped away in their dragonhead boats, disappearing as quickly as they had appeared. This left the English in a state of shock, for they had not believed such a sea attack possible. This success encouraged the Norwegian Vikings to launch more raids against northern England, Scotland, and Ireland. Monasteries were the first targets because they had wealth and few defenses. These small pirate raids were followed by larger, bolder, and better-organized attacks, sometimes with military expeditions with dozens of ships under a commanding chieftain.

Norwegians themselves understand the complexity of the Viking times. Many claim that not all Norwegians of that time should be called Vikings, just the warriors. They point out that most Norwegians were farmers and fisherfolk, who quietly went about their daily lives.

VIKING LIFE Historians tell us that many Viking settlements were based on trade, were well organized, and had a high level of architecture and artistry. They had law assemblies that convened once a year to settle disputes and

Turf houses with sod roofs, like this one in northern Norway, were typical Viking abodes.

make important decisions, although additional meetings could be called to resolve quarrels. Anyone could convene an assembly by sending an arrow to a neighboring farm. One man was selected to memorize the laws and was required to answer anyone who asked a legal question by reciting the appropriate law at the assembly.

VIKING WOMEN Women did the household jobs—mainly cooking, spinning, and weaving—with the help of thralls, or slaves. They also taught their children by telling them stories and riddles, orally passing on their traditions. Viking stories about their heroes, called sagas, were not written down until the thirteenth century.

There was somewhat more equality between the sexes in Viking communities than in the rest of Europe at the time. Viking women could own property, could divorce their husbands, and were in charge when the men were away. A wife's symbol of authority, which she carried fastened to her belt, was the key to the storage chest. The laws from the Viking Age make distinctions between free persons and slaves, but not between men and women. Many Norwegians see a connection between women's solid position during Viking times and their strong social position in Norway today. Norway has had an Equal Status Act since 1976.

ONE NORWAY

Harald Fairhair (ruled 872—930) united most of western Norway after the Battle of Hafrsfjord in 872. (Some historians say it was in 892.) His son Erik Bloodaxe, so called because he murdered seven of his eight brothers, ruled from 930 to 935, and was succeeded by his surviving brother Haakon I Aldalsteinsfostre, also known as Haakon the Good. The new king successfully defeated Erik's sons, who, with aid from their uncle, the king of Denmark Harald Bluetooth, had attempted to overthrow Haakon. Haakon brought Christian missionaries to Norway from England, but his efforts to introduce Christianity to the people failed. He died in battle at Fitjar in 961. Erik's oldest son Harald II Eriksson took the throne and ruled oppressively. Conflict and power struggles erupted, and many regional leaders refused to give up their independence. Sweden and Denmark took advantage of this unrest and invaded Norway.

UNDER DANISH RULE In 995, Olav Tryggvason (ruled 995—1000), the great-grandson of Harald Fairhair, who had been brought up in England and baptized as a Catholic, ascended the throne. Olav I forced Catholicism on the Norwegians. This led Norwegian leaders to ally themselves with the Swedes and Danes to defeat and kill Olav I at the naval Battle of Svolder. The victors divided the land among themselves.

In 1015, another descendant of Harald Fairhair, Olav Haraldsson (ruled 1015—1030), drove out the Swedes and Danes, reunited Norway, and was acknowledged as King Olav II throughout Norway. He continued the Christianization of Norway, using the same ruthless methods as Olav I. As his power grew, he made many enemies among the nobles, who conspired with Canute II of Denmark to overthrow him. Olav II died in 1030 at the Battle of Stiklestad. Norway fell into Danish hands after his death.

This painting of Saint Olav at the Battle of Stiklestad in 1030 was painted by Peter Nicolai Arbo, a Norwegian historical painter, in 1859.

Discontented with Canute's rule, the Norwegians began to think of Olav II as a hero despite his forced Christianization. A year after his death he was proclaimed a saint by the Roman Catholic Church. Saint Olav became the patron saint of Norway, and Christianity firmly rooted itself in the country. When Canute II died in 1035, Olav II's son Magnus was proclaimed Norway's king. Magnus I united Norway and Denmark under his rule in 1047. For the next three centuries, Norwegian kings ruled Norway.

AGE OF GREATNESS

Haakon IV's ascension to the throne (ruled 1217—1263) ended a conflict between the church and the state that began in 1196 and escalated into civil war. He reunited the country and made peace with the church. Then he instituted a new rule of succession ensuring the throne would be passed to the eldest son. Haakon IV's reign is known as the Age of Greatness. He reorganized the government and maintained diplomatic contacts with many countries, including France and England. Under Haakon IV, the kingdom of Norway included all the western islands in the North Atlantic, and mainland Norway contained three regions that are now part of Sweden. Haakon IV also formally annexed Greenland in 1261 and Iceland in 1262.

Haakon was succeeded by his son Magnus Lagabøte. Magnus (Haakon V) revised the laws and persuaded the legislative assemblies to accept a common law for the whole country. When Norway's overseas possessions became hard to defend, Magnus sold the Hebrides and the Isle of Man to Scotland in 1266. This loss of territory signaled the start of the decline of Norway.

UNDER SWEDISH RULE

In 1319 Norway lost its independence when Haakon V died without male heirs. The throne went to the son of his daughter, who had married a Swedish prince. Thus Norway came under Swedish rule. Although Magnus VII ruled over both countries, he only lived in Sweden and neglected Norway.

After the Black Death plague killed half of Norway's population in 1350, the people demanded more consideration of their needs. To satisfy their demands, Magnus VII abdicated in favor of his son Haakon in 1355. Haakon VI would be the last Norwegian king until 1905.

THE KALMAR UNION

Haakon VI's consort, Queen Margrete, who was also queen of Denmark, became queen of Norway when he died in 1380. In 1397, after Swedish nobles elected her to rule their country, Queen Margrete formally united Sweden, Denmark, and Norway under the Kalmar Union. Sweden broke away from the union in 1523, but Norway remained under the Danes for the next four centuries. In 1536, Denmark declared Norway a Danish province, and Norwegians lost the right to influence their country's affairs.

BACK TO SWEDEN

During the Napoleonic Wars of 1804 to 1814, Denmark allied itself with France against Sweden and Great Britain. Britain set up a blockade to prevent ships with supplies from reaching Norway, and the Norwegian people suffered. Denmark, defeated by Sweden in 1813, ceded Norway to Sweden in the Treaty of Kiel, but kept Norway's island colonies—Iceland, Greenland, and the Faeroe Islands.

Norway refused to recognize the treaty. It declared independence and adopted a Norwegian constitution on May 17, 1814. Sweden refused to accept this move and attacked Norwegian troops. In November 1814 the Norwegian parliament accepted King Charles XIII of Sweden as Norway's ruler, and he promised to uphold Norway's constitution. The two countries were to have one king and be allied in war, but in all other respects they were to be independent of each other in full equality. Under the union with Sweden, Norway was granted self-government.

INDEPENDENT NORWAY

The economy in the last few decades of the nineteenth century was good but could not keep pace with the population growth. There was growing unrest, and between 1866 and 1915 more than 600,000 Norwegians emigrated to North America in search of wealth and greater religious freedom. This prompted democratic reforms. The right to vote was extended to all men over the age of twenty-five in 1898 and to women over twenty-five in 1913.

The independence movement had been growing in Norway, and in 1892 negotiations began on the terms of the Swedish-Norwegian union. These proved fruitless, and in 1905 the entire Norwegian cabinet resigned. Norway's constitution only permitted the Swedish king to rule through the cabinet, so this left the king helpless. Norway no longer had a king of its own; therefore the union between Norway and Sweden no longer existed. Sweden initially refused to dissolve the union, but finally agreed to put the matter to a vote in Norway. Norwegians voted almost unanimously for independence, and Sweden recognized Norway as an independent country in September 1905. After establishing independence, Norway declared that it would remain neutral in all international conflicts—a position it would continue during World War I.

The Norwegians voted to establish a constitutional monarchy, and elected Prince Carl of Denmark as their king. He became King Haakon VII of Norway, the first king of Norway since the death of Haakon VI in 1380. He ruled Norway until his death in 1957.

WORLD WAR II

Tensions escalated in Europe during the 1930s. As in World War I, Norway maintained a stance of neutrality. However, neutrality was of little significance when war broke out as both Germany and Britain recognized the strategic importance of Norway—from its coastal bases, German submarines would be able to operate in the North Sea. Realizing this, the Allies announced on April 8, 1940, that the British navy had planted bombs along the Norwegian coast. Norway protested, but soon had worse things to worry about.

THE GERMANS ARE COMING Before dawn on April 9, 1940, the Germans invaded Norway and Denmark in a brilliantly executed surprise attack. Denmark capitulated in a few hours. Norway decided to fight, even though the

Germans were superior in numbers and firepower. In the Oslofjord, Norway's old guns and torpedoes sank the large German cruiser Blücher, killing more than one thousand Germans on board. This delayed the Germans for a few crucial hours, and in that time King Haakon VII and the members of the cabinet and the parliament left Oslo by train for Hamar, 80 miles (129 km) north. The Bank of Norway's 50 tons of gold were also on their way north by the time the Germans overpowered Norway's resistance.

The parliament met in Elverum, Norway, and unanimously decided that the government should have full powers to act on behalf of the nation, even if the king and cabinet were on foreign soil. The Germans demanded that Norway surrender and that King Haakon appoint the founder of the Norwegian Nazi party, Vidkun Quisling, as prime minister. The king declared he would rather abdicate. When the Germans started their bomb raids, the officials hid in the woods nearby. The king and the cabinet fled north, keeping just ahead of the Germans. The provisional capital was set up in the northern city of Tromsø, and then moved to London.

GERMAN OCCUPATION Norway bravely fought the Germans for two months but eventually fell and was occupied until Germany's surrender in 1945. Membership in the Norwegian Nazi party increased from a few thousand in August 1940 to 43,000 in 1943 because of constant pressure to join. Still, Norwegians expressed their resistance to the German occupation in many ways. As a gesture of loyalty to their country, some wore paper clips (a Norwegian invention) on their cuffs or lapels. Others wore flowers in their lapels on patriotic occasions. Many refused to ride buses where they might have to sit next to Germans or Norwegian Nazi party members. Some hid radios to tune in to BBC (Britain's official radio station) broadcasts, and others helped to write and distribute underground newspapers. By 1943, Norway had sixty underground newspapers.

Almost half of Norway's small Jewish population escaped the Nazis. Of the approximately 1,400 Norwegian Jews and 200 Jewish refugees from central Europe, 763 were deported to Auschwitz and other Nazi death or concentration camps. Only twenty-four of the deported Jews survived.

SABOTAGE!

Norwegians mounted many acts of resistance against the Germans. Those ranged from wearing King Haakon VII's emblem to running the Shetland Bus Service that ferried escapees to Scotland and carried weapons, radios, and special agents back to Norway.

One significant act of sabotage was the destruction of the heavy water (deuterium oxide) plant at Rjukan in Telemark, Norway. Heavy water is used in building atomic bombs, and Germany needed this plant in its race against the United States to build the first atomic bomb. On February 27, 1943, nine Norwegians climbed down a steep, icy mountainside, crossed a river, and ascended another dangerous mountain to the heavily guarded factory. Eluding German guards, they broke in, poured out the deuterium oxide, and planted explosives. Four of the nine remained safely hidden on Hardanger Plateau while the Germans mounted an extensive search for the culprits, and the others skied 250 miles (402 km) to safety in Sweden.

The Vemork heavy water plant at Rjukan is now the site of the Norwegian Industrial Workers Museum.

POSTWAR PERIOD

Germany lost the war, and Norway was liberated on May 8, 1945. King Haakon VII returned home to a big welcome. Twenty-four Norwegian collaborators, including Vidkun Quisling, were sentenced to death, and nineteen thousand others were imprisoned. During the Cold War (circa 1947—1991), a period of political tensions between the West and the Soviet Union and Soviet-influenced Eastern Europe following WWII, Norway was anxious because it shared a border with the Soviet Union. Having learned that it could not rely on neutrality, Norway joined the North Atlantic Treaty Organization (NATO) in April 1949.

Norway had been left impoverished in 1945 because no trade was conducted during the war. An acute housing shortage existed because many buildings had been destroyed by retreating German troops and no building construction was started immediately after the war. The government gave priority to restoring Norway's productive capacity in consumer goods. By 1953, the north had been rebuilt and hydroelectric power had increased by 50 percent.

In the late 1960s, oil was discovered in the North Sea off Norway. Oil dramatically boosted the country's economy, transforming Norway from one of Europe's poorest countries to one of its richest. The government put the newfound wealth to good use, building an extensive social welfare system, with free medical care, higher education, and many other robust social benefits. The organized labor movement and the women's movement were also strong contributors to social change during this time. These advances helped turn Norway into one of the most egalitarian social democracies in the world.

TERROR ON AN ISLAND

Norway is known as a peaceful country and doesn't often make news for mass killings. However, in July 2011, one "lone wolf" terrorist conducted two sequential attacks that claimed seventy-seven lives and caused hundreds of injuries. The attacks made enormous news, partly due to the shock factor—they were aimed not only against the government, but also against children—and because they raised important questions about Norway's seemingly inept police response. It was the deadliest attack in Norway since World War II.

Anders Behring Breivik, a thirty-two-year-old right-wing extremist, first exploded a car bomb in Oslo in the government quarter near the office of Prime Minister Jens Stoltenberg. That explosion killed eight people and injured at least 209, but did not hurt the prime minister. Less than two hours later, dressed as a police officer, Breivik attacked a summer camp on the island of Utøya, where 650 young people were staying. There, over a period of an hour and a half, he shot and killed sixty-nine people, of whom thirty-three were under the age of eighteen. The Utøya massacre remains the deadliest shooting worldwide committed by a single gunman.

A report ordered by Norway's parliament found significant delays in communication and response, and that the police could have prevented the bombing, could have arrived on the island sooner, and could have caught Breivik faster. The report said, "All in all, July 22 revealed serious shortfalls in society's emergency preparedness and ability to avert threats.

INTERNET LINKS

www.bbc.com/news/world-europe-17746861
This BBC timeline of Norway's history accompanies a country profile.

www.lonelyplanet.com/norway/history
This travel site offers a good history of Norway.

www.newyorker.com/magazine/2015/05/25/the-inexplicable
This is a fascinating, in-depth portrait of Anders Behring Breivik.

GOVERNMENT

The Norwegian flag flies above the Stortinget in Oslo, the seat of Norway's parliament. The lion is a symbol of Norway.

3

THE KINGDOM OF NORWAY IS a free, independent, indivisible, and inalienable realm. Its form of government is a limited and hereditary monarchy. So reads Article 1 of the Constitution of Norway, as written on May 17, 1814. Article 2 goes on to state, "Our values will remain our Christian and humanist heritage. This Constitution shall ensure democracy, a state based on the rule of law and human rights."

Norway is a constitutional monarchy in which the power is divided between three branches: the legislative, the executive, and the judicial. The constitution was adopted in 1814 but has been revised and amended considerably since then. In 2012, for example, an amendment added a further degree of separation between church and state. As a result, Norway no longer has an official religion, which previously had been the Lutheran Church of Norway.

THE CONSTITUTION

In Norway, the year 1814 is called "the year of miracles." Following Denmark's defeat in the Napoleonic Wars, Norway was ceded to Sweden by the Treaty of Kiel. A council of representatives from all over Norway

The Norwegian flag is red with a blue cross outlined in white that extends to the edges of the flag. The vertical part of the cross is shifted to the hoist side, or the side of the flag nearest the flagstaff, in the style of the Danish flag; the colors recall Norway's past political unions with Denmark (red and white) and Sweden (blue).

met at Eidsvoll and drew up the country's first constitution. They first elected Prince Christian Frederik to be king. He was the Danish vice-regent in Norway who ruled the country on behalf of the Danish King Frederik VI. After an attack by Sweden, however, Christian Frederik realized his cause was lost. He abdicated the throne, but worked to ensure that Norway's newly written constitution would remain intact. The Storting, which is Norway's parliament, met for the first time in Christiania (now Oslo) and adopted the constitution, which had been amended to accept a union with Sweden and the rule of Sweden's Carl XIII.

In the midst of all this, Norway produced what for its time was an extraordinary constitution. It adopted elements of the US constitution, the French constitution of 1791, and constitutional practices in England. It established the principle of the sovereignty of the people and the separation of state powers among executive, judiciary, and legislative branches.

In 2014, Norway—which has been fully independent of Sweden since 1905—celebrated the bicentennial of that constitution. The document was revised so that there are now two equal Norwegian language versions, one in Bokmål and one in Nynorsk, the two written standards of the Norwegian language. In addition a series of human rights articles were added to the constitution.

THE MONARCHY

The king of Norway is a symbol of national unity. He is the head of state, but his power is mainly symbolic. He is also the supreme commander of the Norwegian armed forces and the head of the Church of Norway.

Norway has been blessed with three kind, thoughtful, humble, and good kings since the country's independence from Sweden in 1905. At that time, Norway elected Prince Carl of Denmark as their king. He became King Haakon VII of Norway, the first king of Norway since the death of Haakon VI in 1380. By taking the name Haakon, he resurrected the line that had ended with the death of Haakon VI. King Haakon VII took as his motto "My all for Norway," and the two kings who came after him adopted the same motto.

King Olav V, who ruled from 1957 to 1991, succeeded King Haakon VII. Already a respected resistance hero, Olav soon became admired for his hard work and humble demeanor. Norwegians could even meet him skiing outside Oslo without bodyguards. During the oil crisis in 1972, when the nation was asked to conserve fuel, King Olav set a personal example by taking the trolley when he went skiing and insisting on paying his fare. He holds a special place in the hearts of Norwegians because he made his struggles public. He explained to the people of Norway that he suffered from dyslexia, which made giving speeches a challenge for him. Because he had made this public, the people saw his perseverance as a symbol of human strength.

In 1991, King Olav, more affectionately known as the "people's king," died, and his son, King Harald V, the present king of Norway, succeeded to the throne. The health of the environment is a passion for King Harald. He was president of the World Wildlife Fund before becoming king and often stresses the serious need for worldwide conservation of the environment and Norway's special responsibility as a country with untouched wilderness areas.

Crown Prince Haakon and his father, King Harald V of Norway, pose for an official portrait in 2016.

THE ROLE OF THE ROYAL FAMILY

Royal succession in Norway had long followed the direct male line, but the constitution was changed in 1990, permitting women born after that year to inherit the crown. After Crown Prince Haakon Magnus, who was born in 1973, his first child, Princess Ingrid Alexandra, born in 2004, will accede to the throne.

In addition to royal duties and political affairs, the royal family has always been active in sports, especially skiing and sailing—King Olav won a gold medal for sailing in the Olympics in 1928—and also is very involved in addressing social concerns. Princess Märtha Louise, the oldest daughter of King Harald V and elder sister to Crown Prince Haakon, was appointed a goodwill ambassador by the United Nations High Commissioner for Refugees in 1991.

King Olav, despite the traditional royal reluctance to make public statements seeking to influence policy, made a strong statement in 1987 in favor of maintaining an open society for the increasing stream of refugees into Norway. He reminded the country that he, too, had been an immigrant—arriving in Norway as a two-year-old when most of his family members were in England.

The royal family has had a strong tradition of being close to the people. Although some Norwegians see the monarchy as a contradiction to their ideal of equality, others point out that the king was elected in 1905. Until 1935, however, the Labor government of Norway was unfriendly to the royal family, often refusing to pass the palace budget or to attend dinner parties with the king.

World War II was a turning point in the population's acceptance of the royal family, as Norwegians were impressed with the courage of King Haakon VII in refusing German demands, and the future King Olav's bravery during the resistance. In 2014, 82 percent of Norwegians said they support the country's royal family and the constitutional monarchy. The surprising figures are thought to reflect the highest level of support in several decades.

ADMINISTRATIVE DIVISIONS

Norway is divided into nineteen *fylker* (FEWL-ker), or counties. The city of Oslo is a fylke on its own. Each fylke except Oslo has a governor appointed by the king. The fylker are further divided into rural and urban *kommurer* (koo-MEW-ner), or districts.

Community councils, elected every four years, run the local districts. Each fylke also has a county council consisting of members of the community councils.

From 1938 to 1991, Norway was without a queen. Before 1938, there was Queen Maud, wife of King Haakon VII, who had been frail most of her life. She was the daughter of King Edward VII and Queen Alexandra of Great Britain. Crown Princess Märtha, King Olav's Swedish-born wife and the daughter of Prince Carl of Sweden and Princess Ingeborg of Denmark, subsequently assumed the duties of the queen of Norway, but she died in 1954, before her husband succeeded to the throne. Having been without a queen since 1938, Norwegians were particularly happy when Sonja Haraldsen, a commoner, married Crown Prince Harald and, in 1991, became Norway's first Norwegian-born queen when her husband succeeded to the throne that same year.

Queen Sonja of Norway

THE STORTING

Norway's 169-member parliament (increased from 165 to 169 after the 2005 elections) is called the Storting (stoor-TING) or Stortinget. Only the Storting has the power to enact and repeal laws, amend the constitution, impose taxes, appropriate money for government expenses, and keep a check on government agencies. It also appoints the Nobel Peace Prize committee.

Members of the Storting are elected every four years as representatives of their fylker, or counties, and political parties. Alternates are also elected, in case the elected member dies, is absent, or becomes a member of the cabinet. All Norwegian citizens eighteen years old and older can vote in parliamentary elections. Each of Norway's nineteen counties elects four to seventeen Storting members, depending on the size of the local population.

The Storting is unicameral, meaning it has only one house. In 2009, its two internal chambers, the Lagting (LAHG-ting), or "law assembly," and the Odelsting (OH-duhls-ting), or "heritage of the people assembly," were dissolved.

THE CABINET

The cabinet consists of the prime minister and a number of other ministers (often about eighteen). Most cabinet ministers head a government department such as Foreign Affairs, the Environment, or Church and Cultural Affairs. Cabinet members cannot be members of the Storting, but may be called upon by the Storting to answer questions from the floor of parliament. Cabinet appointments must be approved by the Storting and usually reflect its political composition.

The cabinet meets several times a week. It is generally thought that the Norwegian prime minister, though having considerable influence, has less actual power than the US president or British or Canadian prime ministers.

Erna Solberg became the prime minister of Norway in 2013.

Since 1901 the Nobel Peace Prize committee at the Nobel Institute in Oslo, which consists of five members appointed by the Storting, determines the winner of this prestigious award. The Nobel Peace Prize is given to "the person, or body, who has done the most or the best work for brotherhood among nations, for the abolition or reduction of standing armies, and for the holding and promotion of peace congresses."

Alfred Nobel, the Swedish inventor of dynamite, stipulated in his will of 1895 that the Nobel Prizes in the sciences and for literature should be awarded by Swedish scholarly institutions, but that the decision on the Peace Prize should be left to a committee appointed by the Norwegian parliament.

The Nobel Peace Prize committee considers nominations from Norwegian peace organizations, previous winners, and various other groups. In recent years, nominations have climbed to almost two hundred a year. The committee may refrain from awarding the prize altogether (it has done so nineteen times), may give the prize to one person or institution, or award a joint prize.

Some notable Nobel Peace Prize winners, among the many, have included Martin Luther King Jr. in 1964, the United Nations Childrens Fund (UNICEF) in 1965, Mother Teresa in 1979, the Dalai Lama (Tenzin Gyatso) in 1989, Médecins Sans Frontières (Doctors Without Borders) in 1999, and former US president Jimmy Carter in 2002, "for his decades of untiring effort to find peaceful solutions to international conflicts, to advance democracy and human rights, and to promote economic and social development."

In 2009, newly elected US President Barack Obama won the prize "for his extraordinary efforts to strengthen international diplomacy and cooperation between peoples." At the time, it was considered a controversial choice because he had only just taken office and it seemed premature.

US President Barack Obama displays his Nobel Peace Prize in 2009.

A TIMELINE OF WOMEN'S RIGHTS IN NORWAY

Norway has long been ahead of the times with regard to gender equality and women's rights, both in the social sphere and in politics. The first woman's suffrage organization in Norway was created in 1885, a year after the founding of the first woman's rights association.

1884 . . . *The Norwegian Association for the Rights of Women is founded. It works for improvements in women's education and in the legal status of married women.*

1907 . . . *Norwegian women get limited suffrage in parliamentary elections. All women who pay taxes, or whose husbands pay taxes, may vote.*

1911 . . . *Anna Rogstad becomes the first woman member of the Storting.*

1913 . . . *Norwegian women obtain the right to vote in national elections. Norway is the second country in Europe, after Finland, to extend full voting rights to women.*

Anna Rogstad

1956 . . . *Eva Kolstad becomes president of the Norwegian Association for the Rights of Women, a position she will hold until 1968.*

1960 . . . *Signe Marie Stray Ryssdal becomes Norway's first woman counselor at law.*

1970 . . . *Ragnhild Selmer becomes Norway's first woman Supreme Court judge.*

1971 . . . *Inger Valle becomes Minister of Family and Consumer Affairs.*

1972 . . . *Eva Kolstad becomes Minister of Family and Consumer Affairs and Inger Valle becomes Minister of Government Administration.*

1974 . . . *Eva Kolstad becomes president of the Liberal Party, which was later disbanded.*

1976 . . . *Major Eva Berg becomes chief of the Joint Norwegian Military Nursing Services. Gro Harlem Brundtland becomes Minister of the Environment. Ruth Ryste becomes Minister of Social Affairs. Annemarie Lorentzen becomes Minister of Consumer Affairs and Government Administration. Inger Valle becomes Minister of Justice.*

1978 . . . *Eva Kolstad becomes First Gender Equality Ombud.*

1979 . . . *Norway's Equal Status Act prohibits sexual discrimination in all but religious communities.*

1981 . . . *Gro Harlem Brundtland becomes Norway's first woman prime minister.*

1986 . . . *Gro Harlem Brundtland is reelected as prime minister.*

1988 . . . *The Equal Status Act is amended to require that the percentage of women on all publicly appointed committees and boards must be at least 40 percent.*

1990 . . . *Gro Harlem Brundtland is reelected as prime minister.*

Gro Harlem Brundtland

1990s . . . *The three major political parties, Labor, Center, and Conservative, are headed by women.*

2002 . . . *Private companies are given until 2005 to voluntarily increase the share of women on their boards to at least 40 percent, otherwise sanctions will be imposed.*

2006 . . . *Gender Equality and Anti-Discrimination Ombud position is established to replace earlier Gender Equality Ombud position.*

2013 . . . *Erna Solberg becomes Norway's second woman prime minister.*

POLITICAL PARTIES

Norway has numerous political parties. The Liberal Party is the oldest and was founded in 1884. The Labor Party has been the largest and most often in power since 1927, but over the past three decades it has faced increasing opposition from the Conservatives, who are often allied with the Center Party (formerly the Farmers' Party) and the Christian Democrats. Other parties in Norway include the Socialist Left and the Party of Progress.

Although the Labor Party has traditionally been the party in power, it lost its majority in 1981. Since then, Labor- and Conservative-led minority and coalition parties have alternated being the party in power. These shifts made it increasingly difficult to form stable cabinets because the ruling party must build cabinets through coalitions, and rarely did parties complete their statutory four-year terms until 2001. Coalition parties have held the majority in the Storting since then.

Erna Solberg (right), leader of the Conservative Party, gives a press conference in 2013 along with leaders of other parties about negotiations to form a new conservative coalition government.

INTERNATIONAL COOPERATION

Norway has a tradition of active participation in international organizations that promote peaceful cooperation. Norway is one of four countries that keeps a permanent force of soldiers ready for UN peacekeeping missions and has participated in all of them. Norway was a member of the UN Security Council from 2001 to 2002 and has also been active in the Nordic

Council since the council's founding in 1952. The council coordinates cultural exchange, research, and social welfare benefits among Denmark, Finland, Iceland, Norway, and Sweden. One of the council's most significant results is the freedom of citizens of member countries to travel, work and reside within the member states countries without passports.

In 1994, despite active campaigning in favor of joining the European Union (EU) by the prime minister and other government officials, Norwegians voted for the second time not to join the EU.

INTERNET LINKS

www.cia.gov/library/publications/the-world-factbook/geos/no.html
The CIA World Factbook has up-to-date facts about Norway's government.

nobelpeaceprize.org
This is the site of the Norwegian Nobel committee.

www.nobelprize.org
The official website of the other Nobel Prizes includes information about the Peace Prize as well.

www.regjeringen.no/en/id4
This is the site of the Norwegian government in English.

www.samfunnskunnskap.no/?page_id=395&lang=en
This educational site gives a thorough overview of Norway's government and politics.

www.stortinget.no/en/In-English
The home site of the Storting has excellent information about Norway's government and constitution.

ECONOMY

An abundance of rushing rivers makes Norway a natural location for hydropower. Nearly 99 percent of Norway's power production comes from hydropower.

4

NORWAY HAS A ROBUST ECONOMY with a strong private sector, a large state sector, and an extensive social safety net. It has an abundance of natural resources, including oil and gas, hydropower, fish, forests, and minerals. From 2010 to 2015, the economy enjoyed modest growth.

Norway is one of the world's leading petroleum exporters. The petroleum sector provides about 9 percent of Norway's jobs, 18.6 percent of its gross domestic product (GDP), and makes up 46 percent of its exports, according to official national estimates. Although the government manages the petroleum resources through extensive regulation, the nation is nevertheless vulnerable to changing oil prices. Lower oil prices in 2015, therefore, caused economic growth to slow. However, the government is prepared in such a case. Norway saves state revenue from petroleum sector activities in its Government Pension Fund, the world's largest sovereign wealth fund, valued at over $800 billion as of mid-2015. The government allows itself to use up to 4 percent of the fund's value to help balance the federal budget each year.

All said, Norway's economy is quite healthy. Norwegians enjoy a very high standard of living, even though the country's cost of living is also high. Going forward, however, Norway faces challenges. For one thing, it knows it cannot rely on petroleum-related industries to sustain growth, and it is looking to further diversify its economic base.

Compared to the United States and many European countries, Norwegian employment law is very employee friendly. The Working Environment Act, most recently amended in 2015, regulates matters such as employment, working hours, working age, protection against discrimination, and other employee rights.

OIL AND ENERGY

When Norway sought to extend its territorial waters, geologists testified during hearings in Geneva in 1958 that there was very little possibility of finding oil, gas, or sulfur along Norway's continental shelf. It was not surprising, therefore, that when a representative from Phillips Petroleum in Oklahoma approached former UN Secretary General and Norwegian politician Trygve Lie in 1962 about the possibility of prospecting for oil off Norway, he replied, "I believe you must have made a mistake. Norway has no oil or gas."

In 1969, however, Phillips Petroleum struck oil in what is now known as the Ekofisk oil fields in the Norwegian section of the North Sea. By 1975, Norway was exporting oil products. In 1986 revenues from oil accounted for nearly 20 percent of the GDP, despite a drop in oil prices.

In 2016, Norway was the world's fourteenth largest producer of oil and the third largest exporter of oil after Saudi Arabia and Russia. Most of the current oil resources are located in the continental shelf off Norway's southwestern

The Polar Pioneer, a mobile oil rig, is anchored in Tromsø.

coast, but considerable reserves of oil are known to exist beyond the Arctic Circle. In recent years, the Norwegian government has approved numerous exploratory drilling projects in the Barents Sea and the Norwegian Sea.

The Norwegian government controls much of the oil industry. After the discovery of oil, the Storting voted to limit annual production to conserve the oil fields. In 1972, Statoil, an oil and gas company, was created to oversee all aspects of the oil industry from exploration to processing and the sale of petroleum and natural gas.

Norway has two oil refineries, Mongstad near Bergen and Slagen near Oslo. Most of Norway's oil and gas are exported. Norway provides about 38 percent of Europe's gas requirements. For its own energy, Norway relies heavily on hydroelectric power. Norway produces more hydroelectric power in relation to its population than any other country in the world.

MANUFACTURING

Norway developed industries later than other European countries because it lacked coal to fuel factories. The development of hydroelectric power spurred

Highland cattle, a breed with a double coat of hair, do well in Norway's cold winters.

rapid industrialization in the twentieth century. Early industries depended on local raw materials, such as iron ore, timber, and fish.

In 2015, manufacturing contributed about 8 percent to the country's GDP. About half of Norway's factories are located near Oslo. Higher labor wages in Norway make Norway's products more expensive and less competitive on the international market.

Norway is one of the world's largest exporters of metal. The country imports most of the raw materials it refines and exports these almost immediately after. Norway is one of the world's biggest producers and exporters of chemical products. Other manufactured products include machinery, pulp and paper, and textiles.

AGRICULTURE AND FORESTRY

Norway has only three main farming areas—the southeast, the southwest, and Trøndelag. These areas have a relatively favorable climate, flat fields, and fertile soil. While the total agricultural area remains largely unchanged, the number of farms has decreased from 155,000 in 1969 to fewer than 42,000 in 2015, employing less than 2 percent of the workforce. Most are dairy farms producing milk and cheese. The country produces enough livestock to meet its own needs and grows produce such as potatoes, barley, oats, and wheat.

Norwegian farms are generally small: a typical farm has 22 acres (9 hectares) of arable land and 124 acres (50 ha) of forest. Many farmers supplement their income by engaging in commercial forestry. Land owned by farmers contains about half the nation's productive forests, primarily in the counties of Nord-Trøndelag, Hedmark, Oppland, and Buskerud.

The government has traditionally subsidized farmers. The Storting decided in 1976 that all farmers should have the same annual income as an

A fish farm in Altafjord

average industrial worker. However, these policies are being reviewed, and subsidies have been reduced. The government has promoted a policy of keeping people employed in all rural areas of the country in order to maintain Norway's ability to grow much of its food. As many of the government's agricultural policies are in conflict with the EU's farming regulations, most farmers oppose joining the EU.

FISHING

Providing about 3 percent of the total global catch, Norway ranks as one of the world's top fishing countries, although the industry now earns less than 1 percent of Norway's GDP.

Norwegian fishing crews catch about 2.5 million tons (2.3 million metric tons) of fish per year, including cod, haddock, halibut, coalfish, and shrimp. Most of the catch is processed and exported. Fish farming of salmon and trout in the fjords and coastal inlets has become an important component of the industry. Most of Norway's hatcheries are located in the counties of Hordaland, Møre og Romsdal, and Trøndelag. Aquaculture contributes 25 percent of Norway's total fish production, which in 2009 was 3.9 million tons (3.5 million t) of seafood.

Following a five-year suspension of commercial whaling, Norway resumed minke (a small baleen whale) whaling in 1993. In 2015, Norway killed some 660 minke whales, despite the objections of the International Whaling Commission and numerous whale protection organizations. Norway has consistently fought to retain its right to hunt whales despite falling sales and environmental condemnation.

Seal hunting is still legal, but in 2014, the Norwegian government announced it would stop all subsidies to such hunts due to overwhelming public objection. The subsidies previously accounted for 80 percent of the industry's revenues, so opponents are hoping the move will essentially eliminate seal hunting in Norway.

Seal skins are displayed at a market in Bergen. The skin for 590 kroner would cost about $72.

TRANSPORTATION

Despite its rugged terrain, Norway has developed an efficient network of roads, railways, and water routes. Public transportation is well developed, including intercity buses and streetcars within cities. More than three-quarters of Norway's 57,000 miles (92,000 km) of road are paved. Because of the uneven terrain, many roads curve along fjords and mountains and pass through tunnels and over bridges. The Norwegian road network includes more than five hundred tunnels.

Historically, Norwegians depended on water transport, which was more efficient than land transport, given Norway's physical geography. Coastal passenger and car ferries still provide a vital service for those living in western Norway, where roads are crisscrossed by fjords, and on the hundreds of islands.

Norway's rail system branches out from Oslo and connects all parts of the country. The railway extends to Sweden and Denmark. Norway has about ninety-five airports and relies increasingly on domestic airlines to reach the mountainous areas within the country.

INTERNET LINKS

www.cia.gov/library/publications/the-world-factbook/geos/no.html
The CIA World Factbook has up-to-date statistics on Norway's economy.

www.focus-economics.com/countries/norway
This site evaluates Norway's economic outlook.

www.heritage.org/index/country/norway
The annual Index of Economic Freedom results are found here.

ENVIRONMENT

An electric car gets its battery charged in Oslo.

5

I N 2016, THE ENVIRONMENTAL Performance Index, an annual ranking of countries' performance on high-priority environmental issues, ranked Norway as number 17 out of 180 in the world with a score of 86.9. For comparison, Norway's fellow Scandinavian countries, Finland, Iceland, Sweden, and Denmark, were numbers 1 through 4. The United States came in at number 26.

Norway is one of the least polluted nations on Earth and has few major environmental problems. However, the growth in industrialization and related activities in other nations has exposed Norway's environment to potentially serious damage. In order to protect itself, Norway plays an active role in monitoring and managing ecological issues, not just locally but also internationally.

POLLUTION

Air pollution levels in Norway have been relatively stable over the last decade, with a slight decrease in particulate matter (PM). (Particulate matter is a mixture of extremely small particles and liquid droplets that are suspended in the air. These particles may be dust, soil, soot, smoke, pollen, or other organic or inorganic chemicals, metals, or acids. These materials are considered pollutants and are harmful to human health.)

Norway has the world's largest registered stock of plug-in electric vehicles per capita, with Oslo recognized as the EV capital of the world. In 2014, Norway became the first country where over one in every one hundred passenger cars on the roads is a plug-in electric.

Norway's air pollution levels are similar to those in the other Scandinavian countries, but lower than in southern Europe.

While air pollution in Norway's cities is not as serious as in other major world cities, it is still a concern. One of the most common causes of local pollution is PM and nitrogen dioxide (NO_2). Other components such as sulphur dioxide, ground-level ozone, carbon monoxide, polycyclic aromatic hydrocarbons, and benzene can also contribute to poor local air quality.

Road traffic is the main source of local air pollution in Norway. Partly, this is due to the use of studded snow tires from October to April. A car with studded tires produces up to one hundred times more PM than a car with regular tires. Wood burning stoves also contribute to the levels of PM, especially on cold days, of which Norway has many.

Air pollution is a pervasive problem that does not respect borders. Many hazardous chemicals are carried from afar by air currents and fall as acid rain. The most damaging elements of acid rain are sulfur and nitrogen. About 90 percent of the sulfur and nitrogen that is deposited in Norway comes from other European countries, created by the combustion of fossil fuels. A wide range of measures has been implemented to reduce and limit sulfur and nitrogen emissions. This has substantially reduced pollution, halving the acid rain deposit since 1980. However, despite this success, the damage caused to aquatic animals and plants is taking much longer to repair.

The highly sensitive ecosystems in southern Norway are at particular risk of pollution and erosion from acid rain, mainly because soils there are thin. While levels of heavy metal deposits such as lead have slowly decreased over the past two decades, the effects of mercury levels found in freshwater fish are evident. Contamination of lakes and rivers in the southernmost counties has caused many fish stocks to be depleted, and others such as salmon to be almost completely wiped out. The salmon stocks that survived are now endangered.

Norwegian forests have endured less damage in comparison with the lakes. In 1984, the Norwegian Monitoring Program for Forest Damage was established to keep a check on sulfur and nitrogen fallout. Following a decline in forest conditions due to air pollution and unstable climate in the 1990s, the forests appear to have recovered.

RECYCLING

Since 1995, the total waste volume in Norway has increased by more than 50 percent. In 2013, Norway generated 12.4 million tons (11.2 million t) of waste, an increase of 5 percent over the previous year. Household waste makes up an increasingly larger share of the total—in 2013, households generated 22 percent of all waste in Norway.

The environmental impact of modern waste management depends on the volume and composition of the waste. Landfills can release methane and other greenhouse gases that contribute to global warming. Twenty years ago, most waste was put into landfills in Norway. However, since then, the trend has been recovering and incinerating waste. Incineration can release harmful chemicals and contaminated dust into the atmosphere, although the newest generation of incinerators are the cleanest, and can also generate energy from the waste products. Recovery is the best choice. In 2012, about 81 percent of all waste in Norway was recovered. That means it is extracted for other uses, through recycling, composting, and energy generation. Through legislation, taxes, and economic incentives, homes, businesses, and industries are continually encouraged to practice environmentally-friendly waste recovery to reduce these harmful effects on the environment.

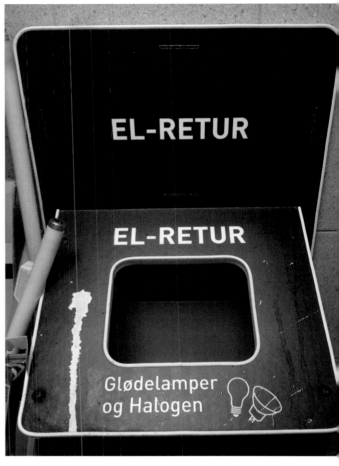

A collection bin for used electronics encourages recycling in a Norwegian grocery store.

POLAR REGION

Once a virtually untouched wilderness, the Arctic is now under pressure from growing human invasion. As industry and tourists head deeper into the Arctic, monitoring and preserving this very fragile environment has become essential.

Svalbard's distinct landscape and ecosystem remain largely intact thanks to stringent measures aimed at protecting territories and natural species. The Svalbard Environmental Protection Act was implemented in 2001 with strict regulations to protect nature and historical sites. Under the act, all traces of human activity from 1945 or earlier are considered protected cultural remains. With 56 percent of Svalbard's land area protected, further conservation plans were passed in 2002, and again updated in 2014, to extend legal protection by transforming other biologically productive areas into nature reserves.

Pollution in Norway's Arctic region comes mainly from distant sources. However, locally used organic environmental toxins such as polychlorinated biphenyls (PBC) and plant-protecting products have damaging effects on the reproductive system of mammals. Accumulated amounts of these toxins have been discovered in species at the end of the Arctic food chain, such as the polar bear, and seal around Svalbard, and these levels of toxins are among the highest in the Arctic.

Another major concern is global warming. Reports by the UN Panel on Climate Change warn that global warming will cause temperatures in the Arctic to rise more than the global average. The rise in temperature can cause substantial amounts of sea ice to melt and land such as Greenland in the Arctic Circle to flood due to the rise in the sea level. This can result in devastating consequences such as the contamination of freshwater supplies, coastal flooding, and unpredictable weather patterns.

MARINE LIFE

Just as pollution is a threat to Norway's rivers, lakes, and coastal areas, it has become evident over the past decade that it also has an impact at sea. Cold-water coral reefs found along the entire coastline of Norway and located about 6,562 feet (2,000 m) deep, are important for the ecosystem. They are crucial for fisheries, research, and marine resources, but they are the most vulnerable of marine environments. Between 30 percent and 50 percent of coral reefs in Norwegian waters have been damaged or crushed by trawling activities.

In recent years authorities have taken measures to protect coral reefs. According to the World Wildlife Fund (WWF) in 2003, Norway is the only country to have implemented protection measures for cold-water reefs in European waters. That same year the WWF presented Norway its highest award for global conservation—the International Gift to the Earth Prize—in recognition of Norway's efforts in successfully stemming the deterioration of Norwegian coral reefs.

PROTECTED LAND

Forests and other woodlands cover 39 percent of Norway's land area, amounting to about 30 million acres (12 million ha). Approximately 88 percent of this is privately owned, divided among more than 120,000 properties. Legislation, taxation, and economic support programs are in place to promote forest production and to sustain the forest as a thriving environment for plants, animals, and human recreation. To encourage optimal use of forest resources, and to reduce the use of fossil fuels, the government launched a five-year development program in 2000 aimed at promoting wood as an environmentally-friendly material suitable for a wider range of applications.

A waterfall cascades from a glacier in Jostedalsbreen National Park.

About 25 percent of total forest area is protected in order to safeguard natural resources, soil, and water against normal hazards and extreme climate conditions. Protected forests fall into several categories, including forest reserves and national parks.

There are forty-four national parks in Norway, thirty-seven on the mainland, and seven on Svalbard. In 1962, the Norwegian state started creating national parks with the purpose of preserving the rich diversity of the country's wildlife and natural environments, from the fjords to the mountains. The Norwegians are protective and proud of their parks as they view outdoor recreation as a large part of their cultural identity.

Visitors to the parks have opportunities to experience and admire wonderful varieties of plant, bird, and animal life. They can also hike

Outdoor recreation is a big part of Norwegian culture. Everyone in Norway has public right of access to any uncultivated land in the countryside. This is according to an ancient unwritten law called allemannsretten *(AWL-leh-mawns-reht-ten), or "every man's right." It is thought to date way back to the Viking age.*

There is no law about this right, only restrictions that are outlined in the Outdoor Recreation Act. People are free to ramble through forests, hike up mountains, ski, cycle, or swim anywhere as long as no harm or disturbance is caused. This right also extends to cultivated land when it is frozen or snow-covered but does not apply if one is using a motor vehicle or engaging in sport fishing and hunting. With this freedom comes every individual's obligation to respect the natural environment.

In recent years increased commercial development has posed a threat to rights of access, particularly along coastal areas where homes and holiday cabins are being built. In response, the government is taking steps to safeguard the people's right to enjoy the natural landscape.

through valleys and glaciers and enjoy panoramic views of the country's diverse and distinct landscapes. These include the gently rolling mountains of Hardangervidda, Norway's largest national park; northern Europe's highest peaks, at Jotunheimen National Park; and Europe's largest glacier, at Jostedalsbreen.

CULTURAL HERITAGE

Preserving Norway's heritage involves the protection of monuments, sites, and cultural environments. About 58,000 archaeological sites containing about 300,000 monuments have been registered in Norway. Each year about 1 percent of these are lost or damaged.

Norway's architectural heritage includes 375,000 buildings registered as being one hundred years old or more, although only a small percentage is protected by the Cultural Heritage Act. Those that are protected include stave churches and other medieval wooden buildings.

Norway also extends protection of individual monuments and structures to include the surrounding environment. There are currently four such protected areas: the Havrå farm complex, the Ustein monastery, Kongsberg Silver Works, and the Sami settlement, Neiden. Other projects have been undertaken to safeguard important areas along the coast as well as restoration works.

Seven Norwegian sites are on UNESCO's World Heritage List. These are the rock drawings of Alta, Urnes Stave Church, Bryggen (the old wharf) in Bergen, the mining town in Røros, the Struve Geodetic Arc (a chain of survey triangulations stretching from Norway to the Black Sea), and the Vega Archipelago. The Rjukan-Notodden Industrial Heritage Site was added in 2015.

INTERNET LINKS

www.environment.no
The Norwegian Environment Agency provides information in English with statistics, articles, and maps.

www.fjordnorway.com/things-to-do/natural-attractions/national-parks
This site has photo galleries of several of Norway's national parks.

travel.nationalgeographic.com/travel/parks/svalbard-norway
This is a quick overview of the national parks of Svalbard.

www.nytimes.com/2013/04/30/world/europe/oslo-copes-with-shortage-of-garbage-it-turns-into-energy.html?_r=0
This is an article about how Norway imports waste to turn into energy.

whc.unesco.org/en/statesparties/no
This UNESCO page lists and describes Norway's properties on the World Heritage List.

NORWEGIANS

This smiling, fair-haired woman happens to fit the stereotypical appearance of Norwegians, but not all Norwegians do.

ALL NORWEGIANS ARE FAIR-SKINNED, blonde, blue-eyed people. They wear thick-knit sweaters, eat pickled fish and reindeer meat, and ski all the time without ever getting cold. Of course, that isn't true—it's a stereotype. Like most stereotypes, however, it carries a kernel of truth. Norwegians and other Scandinavians have the highest percentage of blondes in the world, but this certainly doesn't mean everyone is light-haired.

Most Norwegians are closely related to the Danes and the Swedes. The ancestors of these three Scandinavian peoples came from lands east of the Baltic Sea, from around the Mediterranean Sea, or from the European Alps. Over the centuries, Norwegians have intermarried with other groups. Icelanders are largely descended from Norwegian migrants to medieval Iceland. Many people living in northern Scotland and the islands of Orkney and Shetland are partially descended from Norwegian settlers as well.

6

A total of 59,058 children were born in Norway in 2015. The average age of the mother was 28.9 years, and the father's average age was 31.4. A woman's age at the birth of her first child is trending older. The average age in 1990 was 25.5 years. The number of women having three or more children is going down. In 2015, 30.7 percent of Norwegian women had given birth to three or more children; in 2005, it was 34.8 percent.

NORWEGIAN FINNS

The Kvener, or Finns, were involved in trade in northern Norway from the early twelfth century. From the early eighteenth century through the nineteenth, some Finns came to Norway, looking for a more secure life in the fjords of Troms and Finnmark. Some were escaping skirmishes with Russians. Others were fleeing the Swedish wars and the famine years of the 1860s. The best known Kven center, Vadsø

Finnish is still spoken in some households in Vadsø, in Finnmark, Norway.

on the far northeastern coast of Norway, was called Vesi-Saari in Finnish, meaning "water island." In 1875, Finnish speakers made up 62 percent of the population, but today very little Finnish is heard in Norway.

THE SAMI

The Sami (sometimes called Lapps or Lapplanders) have lived in Norway, Sweden, Finland, and the Kola Peninsula of Russia for thousands of years. Originally from Asia, they are of a darker complexion and are shorter than most Norwegians. Their language is related to Finnish. Because there is no overall registration of the Sami population, no one knows exactly how many Sami there are today, and estimates vary quite a bit. According to Statistics Norway, some thirty-eight thousand Sami are thought to live in Norway. The CIA World Factbook reports sixty thousand. Whatever their number, they are the country's indigenous people.

More than half of the Norwegian Sami live in the northern county of Finnmark—its name means "Sami borderland." In Old Norse, the Sami were called Finner, a reference to their ability to find their way in wild country. Traditionally, the Sami are nomads who follow herds of reindeer. Many

There are more than 100,000 reindeer, both domesticated and wild, in Northern Norway. The life of the Sami reindeer-herding nomads has a regular pattern: a long stay at a winter base where herds feed on lichen under snow and on trees, a spring migration toward the coast with a pause for calving, a search for and travel to grazing areas on peninsulas and islands during summer, and in the fall, a reindeer roundup before heading back to camp. Nomadic Sami live in lavvo *(LAH-voh), traditional skin tents, and travel on skis, the most efficient way of traversing snowy areas.*

Over the years, reindeer-herding Sami have faced serious obstacles when their traditional migration routes have been threatened and disrupted by dams, roads, national parks, sport fishing and hunting, mining, tourism, and military bases. Pollution is also a serious threat. The Chernobyl nuclear explosion in 1986 in Ukraine affected the Sami living in Trøndelag, as they were forced to slaughter their herds due to the high level of radioactivity caused by particulate fallout blown in by winds.

The Alta-Kautokeino River hydroelectric project proposed in 1970 became a major test of Sami rights. Sami, environmentalists, and advocates for ethnic and minority rights agitated against the dam, which would affect traditional Sami migratory routes. Despite the high level of mobilization against the project, the Storting and the Supreme Court approved it in 1982, and it was completed in 1987.

The issue of land rights became a controversial issue in the 1990s. In 2005, as a result of Sami activism, the Norwegian parliament passed the Finnmark Act. It transferred about 95 percent (about 46,000 sq km) of the land and water in Finnmark to the inhabitants of the county, whether Sami or Norwegian. The Sami Parliament and the Finnmark Provincial Council have a joint responsibility to administer the region, which no longer belongs to the Norwegian state.

modern Sami have settled in fishing and farming communities, and many of them marry other Norwegians.

Like Native Americans, the Sami are eager for outsiders to see beyond the stereotypes based on museum displays and early travelers' accounts. The Romans recorded that the Sami dressed in animal skins and traveled on narrow pieces of wood—the earliest skis—and that Sami women hunted alongside the men. In the fifteenth century, Norwegians began to invade Sami areas, depleting stocks of wild game. Some Sami responded by becoming full-time reindeer breeders and herders and organizing cooperatives based on kinship ties. Others settled on the coast and obtained food by hunting and fishing. Today only about 10 percent of the Sami are reindeer herders.

Only two-thirds of the Sami speak a Sami dialect, an unfortunate result of attempts by missionaries, agricultural experts, and schoolteachers from the 1850s to the 1950s to "Norwegianize" the Sami. In the 1960s, the official government position shifted to a policy of accommodation and support. Research projects focusing on the Sami language and culture resulted in new curricula for all educational levels. Today, students may choose Sami as their first language in many communities. The Sami themselves have become involved in this Sami revivalism. There are now Sami newspapers, a Sami radio station, a major research library housed in Karasjok, and museums and theater groups. In 1989, the Sami parliament was established, giving Sami people a voice in issues concerning their interests in Norway.

THE ROLE OF WOMEN

Traditionally, Norwegian women have fended for themselves and made their own decisions. In many rural communities the men used to go fishing off the coast for several months, leaving the women to run the farms and local affairs. This pattern continues today, with the men going off to work on oil rigs for two to three weeks at a time before returning home for a couple of weeks—except that today there are also women working on the rigs, and most women onshore are no longer on farms.

Even though Norway was the second country to give women the right to vote in national elections, and the first woman to sit in the Storting was

From 1840 until World War I, a growing flood of emigrants left Norway for the New World. Most emigrated because of rural poverty, leaving behind them small huts that have been called starvation cottages. Many were farm laborers who were paid only a few pennies a day, or children of farmers whose plots were too small or infertile to support an extended family.

Before the US Immigration Act of 1924 restricted the flow of refugees, more than 800,000 Norwegians had migrated to the United States. In 1882 alone, 28,628 Norwegians emigrated. No other country, except Ireland, had larger numbers of its people moving to the United States.

Most Norwegians settled in the Midwestern states, especially the farming communities of Wisconsin and Minnesota. Life in the early years was hard for these immigrants, but Norwegian-language newspapers, churches, and cultural associations helped keep the

In this photo from 1906, Norwegians wave goodbye to relatives emigrating to America.

communities together. Today, at least two private US colleges have Norwegian roots: Saint Olaf College in Northfield, Minnesota, and Luther College in Decorah, Iowa.

A number of private and public organizations have been founded to help Americans interested in researching their family history and lineage. Today, there are as many people of Norwegian descent living in the United States as there are Norwegians in Norway. Some three million Americans consider their ancestry to be completely or mainly Norwegian, and another 1.5 million claim partial Norwegian ancestry. There are also many people descended from Norwegians in Canada and Australia.

Anna Rogstad in 1911, no woman became a cabinet minister until 1945, when Kirsten Hansteen was given the title of consultant minister but without a department to run.

Norwegian women entered the paid workforce later than other Scandinavian women. Even with the Equal Status Act, there remains differences in pay and the sharing of housework. However, with the gap between working hours of men and women closing, surveys show that women in Norway spend less time on housework today than forty years ago. Many Norwegian women have also traditionally chosen to be educated within the caring professions, such as public health and social welfare. This has given rise to strong patterns of occupational segregation, and today few women hold high-level jobs in industry or banking.

The University of Oslo has the world's first Institute for Women's Law—a major research organization for women sponsors studies of issues that affect and concern women. The university also started the Center for Women's Studies and Gender Research in 1997.

NEWCOMERS

In recent years there has been a dramatic increase in the number of immigrants moving to Norway. In 2015, they made up 15.6 percent of the population. Norway's high standard of living, stable government, and relatively peaceful society have made it a popular destination for people fleeing war-torn, politically oppressive, or economically depressed countries.

Norway has a strong tradition of offering a home to asylum seekers and refugees. In 2015 alone, 31,145 refugees—mainly from Syria, Iraq, and Afghanistan—sought asylum in Norway. Wars in those three countries caused a mass exodus of emigrants, and Europe faced the biggest refugee crisis since 1945.

Norway provides schooling in the foreigner's native language, but newcomers are expected to learn Norwegian. School-age immigrants are expected to attend school. Others are integrated through work programs and Norwegian language classes. Most immigrants live in Oslo or near Bergen and

Stavanger. While most Norwegians are comfortable with ethnic and cultural diversity, many expect non-Western immigrants to assimilate quickly into the Norwegian way of doing things. Some foreigners have experienced discrimination because of this expectation.

Recognizing that Norway is changing, the government has begun to set up agencies to address immigrant issues, provide assistance to minorities, and to bridge cultural barriers.

Roma immigrants from Romania demonstrate in front of City Hall in Oslo.

INTERNET LINKS

www.cia.gov/library/publications/the-world-factbook/geos/no.html
This site lists population and demographic statistics for Norway.

ngm.nationalgeographic.com/2011/11/sami-reindeer-herders/benko-text
"Scandinavia's Sami Reindeer Herders" is an article with an extensive, captioned photo gallery and video.

www.nordnorge.com/en/sapmi
This site about Northern Norway has numerous articles about the Sami people.

www.ssb.no/en
Statistics Norway has up-to-date facts about Norwegian society in English.

LIFESTYLE

A pregnant woman basks in the sunshine on her trek to the Nigardsbreen glacier in Norway.

NORWAY ENJOYS ONE OF THE HIGHEST living standards in the world. There isn't the wide discrepancy in income that is seen in other nations because the taxation system takes from the wealthy and gives to the not-so-wealthy. This has resulted in a fairly equitable society where most people are in roughly the same economic class.

WORK

Norwegians are a hardworking people who also know where their priorities lie. Norway's parliament passed a Worker's Protection Act that limits maximum working hours to an annual average of nine hours a day. All night work is prohibited for day workers, as is working on Sundays and public holidays.

Child labor is strictly controlled, and children under the age of fifteen are allowed only light work, such as that of messengers. Those under the age of eighteen are not permitted to work overtime or at night.

Usual business hours are from 8 a.m. to 4 p.m., with only a short break of about twenty minutes for lunch, usually of sandwiches brought from home. These working hours are faithfully followed in winter, but in summer, office workers often leave work an hour earlier in order to enjoy the sun as much as possible. Norway has also legislated a four-week vacation with full pay for all workers. This means workers can enjoy more time for family activities and leisure pursuits. Striking a balance between family time and work is a deliberate policy in Norway. Both parents can share forty-two weeks of fully paid leave when they have a baby. The father has to take at least four weeks of these or forfeit them.

A WELFARE NATION

Norway is a world leader in state-funded health care, housing, employment benefits, retirement plans, and other services. Norwegian laws guarantee the right to employment, a place to live, education, social security, and health and hospital benefits. The welfare system is funded through taxes and insurance. Recently, however, there has been discontent with the high level of taxation, and Norwegians have begun to question whether they want to continue subsidizing lower-income families, usually immigrants.

Families with children under eighteen receive a yearly allowance per child, while single parents receive benefits for one child more than is actually supported. Aid is also available to help these families pay for housing. This has ensured a minimum standard of living for all Norwegian citizens.

Norwegians are required to buy into the social security national insurance program, which includes retirement funds, job retraining, and unemployment benefits. Free medical care and disability benefits are part of the plan. The cost of the program is borne jointly by workers, employers, and national and local governments.

HEALTH

Norwegians have no severe health problems apart from those common to wealthy countries, namely heart disease and cancer. Children receive a program of vaccinations, and everyone undergoes periodic tests for tuberculosis.

In 2015, the average life expectancy at birth for Norwegians was 81.7 years, a gain of almost 30 years over their ancestors in the 1890s, who could only expect to live for 52 years, on average. Norway also has one of the lowest infant mortality rates in the world, at 2.48 deaths out of every 1,000 babies born in 2015. Norway is now experiencing a shortage of retirement and nursing homes because more Norwegians are living longer. Officials have projected that the number of persons aged sixty-seven years and older will double between 2002 and 2050. As with most industrialized countries, Norway has a very low birth rate. More women who choose to conceive are content with just having one or two children.

MARRIAGE

Weddings in Norway look much like weddings in the United States or other European countries, with the bride wearing a long white or silver dress and the groom wearing a tuxedo. However, some couples choose to go with the old traditions. In that case, the groom wears a special outfit called a *bundas*. This suit harkens back to centuries past, with its top coat, vest, short pants, and stockings. The colors of the suit differ from region to region, and are worn with great pride. The bride wears a *brudekjole*, a traditional woven costume—typically a dress with an apron over it—which also reflects her

An illustration from 1860 shows a traditional Norwegian wedding procession.

heritage. On her head she wears a *brudekrone*, or bridal crown, of silver and gold. The elaborate crown is decorated with bangles that make a melodic tinkling sound when the bride moves her head. In the old days, this sound was thought to ward off evil spirits, but today it just adds to the merriment.

In a small town, the bridal party will walk to the church in a procession led by fiddlers. During the ceremony, the couple will exchange rings—but in Norway, the wedding ring is traditionally worn on the right hand.

Same-sex marriage became legal in Norway in 2009. That year, Norway became the first Scandinavian country and the sixth country in the world to legalize same-sex marriage. In 2016, the Church of Norway voted in favor of allowing same-sex marriages.

BIRTH AND BAPTISM

Although women do visit clinics for prenatal care before their babies are born, they turn to midwives to help them through the nine months of pregnancy. When it is time for the baby to be born, the local midwife accompanies the woman to the hospital and places her into the care of the hospital midwife, who supervises the birth.

One of the first ceremonies many children undergo is baptism. Baptism marks the child's entry into the Lutheran Church of Norway. Family and close friends are usually invited, and two married couples are selected as the child's godparents. Theirs is a lifelong task as they are expected to be the child's moral guides, to ensure that he or she grows up with sound values and tolerant attitudes. The number of children being baptized each year is falling, however. In 2015, only 57.8 percent of children born in Norway were baptized, more than 8 percent fewer than in 2011.

Baptism is also the ceremony at which a child is named. Naming a child in Norway used to follow a strict pattern. The eldest son was named after his paternal grandfather, and the next son after his maternal grandfather. The eldest and second daughters were named after their paternal and maternal grandmothers, respectively. Then the names of great-grandparents were used, or relatives who had passed away. Today, however, Norwegians are free to choose their children's names. They may make the selection from a

The kvinnegruppe (KVIN-nuh-GREW-puh) is a gathering of women interested in discussing women's issues and current literature. Members are mostly professional women in their mid-twenties to mid-thirties, although many are homemakers and university students. The groups are not action-oriented, but serve as an outlet for women to discuss matters that concern them and to listen to other women's points of view. It is also a wonderful opportunity for interaction with like-minded women, and most members enjoy relaxing with a cup of coffee in a pleasant atmosphere. Some groups are aimed at helping immigrant women practice Norwegian and learn about women's lives in Norway. There is a kvinnegruppe in almost every district.

Women's groups are not restricted to the kvinnegruppe. The husmorlag (HEWS-moor-lahg) is a neighborhood group of women who do projects of common interest: running preschool centers; helping the elderly; doing charity work; or learning a language. Notices of their activities are posted in community centers, churches, and neighborhood stores.

book of names, or name their children after friends or relatives. Often a child is given a grandparent's name as his or her middle name.

CONFIRMATION

This is one of the most important ceremonies for Norwegians who belong to the Church of Norway. Confirmation represents a fourteen- or fifteen-year-old's acceptance of a Christian heritage and the principles of the Lutheran Church of Norway.

All those wishing to be confirmed attend a two-month preparatory course, during which they are given a thorough grounding in the principles of the church. If they decide they can abide by these principles, they then go through the confirmation ceremony, in which they publicly declare that they wish to remain a part of the Lutheran Church. The confirmation ceremony takes place in church and is attended by friends and family. There is usually a large celebration after the ceremony, and friends and relatives come from all over to participate in the occasion and celebrate with the family.

THE COMMISSIONER FOR CHILDREN

In the 1970s, parliamentary debate on how the country could best address children's needs in a democracy where children have no vote resulted in the creation of the children's ombudsman, the Commissioner for Children.

The ombudsman's duties are to promote the interests of children and to monitor the conditions under which children grow up. The ombudsman comes under the Ministry for Children and Family Affairs. The work is twofold: gathering information from all levels of society and then approaching the authorities with problems, criticisms, and proposals for change.

The ombudsman has a high public profile as the children's spokesperson on issues important to them. On a radio and television show, the ombudsman reads out the latest cases handled and letters received from children about issues as diverse as dangerous play areas and living in families with alcoholics.

EDUCATION

As education is free up to university level, virtually everyone in Norway can read and write. Children in Norway begin school at age seven, and basic education lasts nine years. Children go through six years of elementary education, followed by another three years in junior high school. In order to ensure that all Norwegian children have equal educational opportunities, the Norwegian school system decides on one elementary curriculum and one method of teaching for the entire country. The curriculum focuses on nature study, physical education, social studies, and Christianity, in addition to math, science, Norwegian, and foreign languages.

After junior high many students proceed to three years of high school education. This could be obtained at a gymnasium, which focuses on general education in preparation for a course of study at a university, or a vocational school for occupational training.

Norway has six universities, located in Oslo, Trondheim, Bergen, Tromsø, Ås, and Stavanger. The country has several colleges, all funded by the state.

HOUSES AND GARDENS

Many Norwegians living in cities join housing cooperatives called *borettslag* (BOOR-ehts-lahg), which finance housing projects. Single residences or apartments are then rented to its members, who pay a deposit to join in addition to the monthly rent. It is a first-come, first-served system, and some Norwegian parents sponsor their children's membership in a borettslag years before it is needed in order to give them an early start in the waiting line. If a member wishes to leave such a cooperative and to sell his or her share in it, the board of the cooperative must approve the sale.

Row houses and condominiums are popular in urban areas, and single houses are common in the country. Summer homes near the sea or in the mountains are popular with urban Norwegians. These are usually simple shacks with a garden where the family enjoys outdoor meals in fine weather.

Norwegians have a reputation for being self-sufficient, particularly when work is to be done in their own house or garden. Tasks such as painting, wallpapering, or fixing the roof are tackled with relish. Most cities have a local gardening association and plant nurseries that give seasonal planting advice. In Oslo a public area is set aside for those who wish to indulge in summer gardening.

INTERNET LINKS

mylittlenorway.com/2010/06/why-live-in-norway
This post gives in-depth, practical information on many aspects of daily life in Norway.

www.telegraph.co.uk/expat/life/is-norway-really-the-most-liveable-place-on-earth
This article describes the Norwegian lifestyle for expats.

www.womenshealthmag.com/food/healthy-lifestyle
"Healthy Habits in Norway" is an interesting article about Norway's healthy lifestyle.

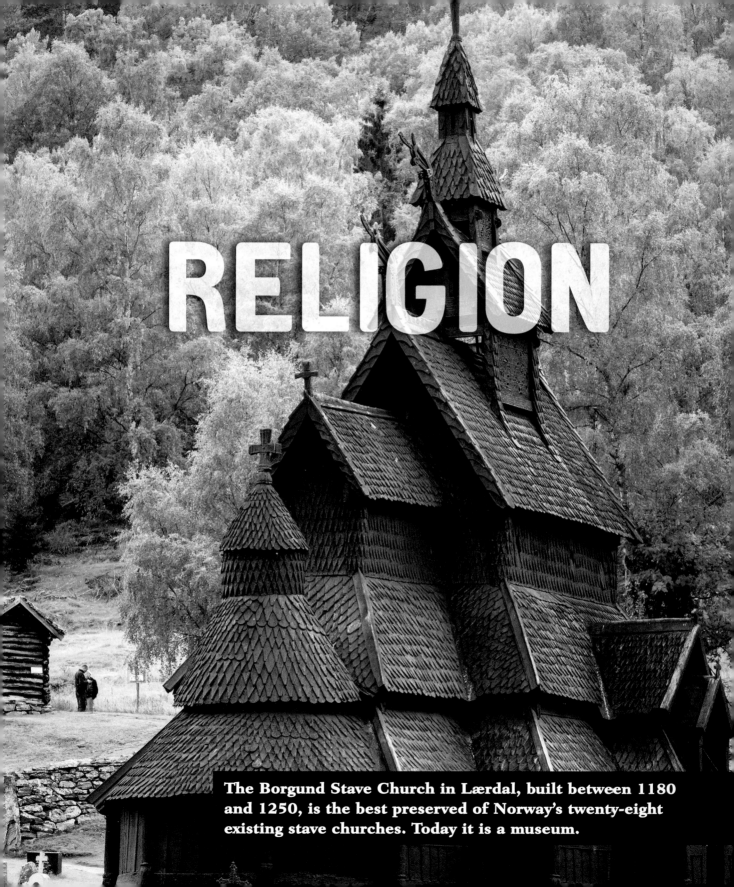

RELIGION

The Borgund Stave Church in Lærdal, built between 1180 and 1250, is the best preserved of Norway's twenty-eight existing stave churches. Today it is a museum.

8

NORWAY IS AN OVERWHELMINGLY Christian nation. Almost 90 percent of Norwegians are Christian, and of these, 76 percent are members of the Evangelical Lutheran Church of Norway. Until 2012, the Church of Norway was the country's official state church, but that year the Norwegian parliament changed the constitution to enact more of a separation between church and state.

Despite those figures, Norway has seen a great decline in religiosity in recent years, at least among native-born Norwegians. This trend follows much of Europe, where atheism and agnosticism are common and increasingly popular philosophies. The majority of Norwegian Lutherans are baptized, confirmed, married, and buried in religious ceremonies, but fewer than 20 percent of Norwegian adults attend church more than five times a year.

Although these figures appear to be contradictions, they aren't necessarily. Many Norwegians may identify as Christians in terms of their cultural heritage. They may celebrate the Christian holidays—they might even attend services—while simultaneously having personal questions of belief and philosophy.

According to a 2016 survey conducted annually since 1985, the number of Norwegians who say they do not believe in God has topped the number of those who do believe for the first time ever. The poll of four thousand Norwegians, conducted by Ipsos MORI for the Norwegian Monitor, revealed that 39 percent claim to be atheists, compared to 37 percent of believers. The remaining 23 percent said they did not know.

THE CHURCH OF NORWAY

The origins of the Lutheran Church go back to Martin Luther (1483—1546), a German Catholic priest who objected to some Catholic practices and started the revolution known as the Protestant Reformation. Through his actions and writings, Luther ushered in not only Protestantism, but also conditions for a revolution in economic, political, and social thought.

By the mid-sixteenth century most of northern Europe was Lutheran. Lutheranism reached Denmark as early as the 1520s, but it was not until 1539 that the Danish Church was established with the king as the head and the clergy as leaders in matters of faith. As it was part of the Kalmar Union with Denmark and Sweden at the time, Norway followed suit.

Lutherans, like other Protestant denominations, believe in the divinity and humanity of Jesus Christ and in the Trinity of God. They have two sacraments—baptism and the Lord's Supper (or communion). The congregation is led by either a pastor or a lay person, who is elected from the membership of a council made up of a congregation's clergy and elected lay persons.

The Church of Norway is still partially state funded, and the government appoints pastors and church officials. In 1956 the Storting passed a law allowing women to become pastors; the state named the first female pastor in 1961.

NORWAY'S CONVERSION TO CHRISTIANITY

During their expeditions overseas, the Vikings came in contact with Christian Europe. Some Vikings pretended to convert in order to get trade benefits, but those who settled abroad usually became Christians. Norway, however, remained faithful to the old gods for a long time. Christianizing the country took two hundred years and was marked by much bloodshed.

THE MISSIONARY KING Before his death, Harald Fairhair bequeathed the realm to his son Erik Bloodaxe (ruled 930—935). When Erik was forced from

OLD NORSE GODS

The mythology of northern Europe goes back to a time long before the Vikings. Viking poets and storytellers retold many tales, often with conflicting details, about the gods and goddesses who lived in a heavenly place called Asgard.

Chief among the pagan gods were Odin (or Woden), god of war and wisdom; Thor, the god of thunder and storms and the slayer of trolls and giants; Frey, the god of fertility and peace; Tyr, the bravest fighter among them all; and Freya, the Earth goddess and patron of pleasure.

Odin was the god of poetry and magic as well as war, and the early kings of Norway were fond of tracing their ancestry back to him. Odin sent young women called Valkyries to lead warriors who had died in battle to the Viking heaven, Valhalla. This was a huge hall with 640 doors, each so wide that 960 einherjer (EIN-hair-yair), meaning "former warriors," could pass through them side by side.

Odin, who had sacrificed one of his eyes in exchange for a drink from the Well of Knowledge, had two ravens, Hugin and Mugin. The birds set out each dawn to fly all over the world and returned every night to report on all that had happened during the day. Odin's wife, Frigg, the mother goddess, spun gold thread on her spinning wheel that she wove into summer clouds on her loom.

Although Odin was the chief god, Thor was more popular because of his power over the weather. His symbol was the hammer, with which he made the great noise of thunder. Frey, the god of fertility and harvest, had to be appeased by the Vikings. To please Frey they scattered bread and poured wine on the ground when they sowed their seeds.

A statue of King Olav Tryggvason stands in Trondheim.

the throne, Harald's younger son, Haakon (ruled 945—960), who was only fifteen, returned to Norway and united most of the country.

Haakon, who had been educated as a Christian at the court of King Athelstan in England, was Norway's first Christian king, and he wanted Norway to become a Christian country. He was so well liked that he was called "Haakon the Good." However, he made little headway in establishing Christianity.

OLAV TRYGGVASON The grandson of Harald Fairhair, Olav Tryggvason, claimed the throne of Norway in 995. As a child, he fled to Russia with his mother to escape from being killed by Erik Bloodaxe. From there, he began a career as a Viking at an early age, conducting raids from the Baltics to the British Isles. Olav was so famous that he was able to collect large fleets of ships for his part in Viking attacks against England in the 980s and 990s. In England he accepted Christianity and was confirmed by the Bishop of Winchester under the sponsorship of King Æthelred the Unræd (or Ethelred the Unready)—whom he had recently attacked. When he arrived in Norway in 995, Olav was immediately accepted as king in Trøndelag, though more gradually by the rest of the country.

Aided by English missionaries, Olav was determined to bring Christianity to the people of Norway. Around the year 1000, he sent a Catholic priest with Viking Leif Eriksson to Greenland to convert the settlers. Many of the settlers converted, but for Olav, in Norway, conversion was a struggle. Many Norwegians still believed in the old gods, and so Olav resorted to force. Using the methods of a Viking raider, Olav sailed along the coast demanding that the *tings*, or assemblies, submit and accept baptism. Those who refused were tortured or put to death. He forbade the worship of the old gods, destroyed their temples, and built the first church in Norway, in a village in Moster, south of Bergen. Olav's methods gained him many enemies and he was killed at the Battle of Svold in 1000.

NORWAY'S ETERNAL KING Olav Haraldsson began his Viking career when he was twelve years old. He fought in the Baltics, in Western Europe, and in England, where in 1009 he attacked London and helped to tear down London Bridge with grappling irons. This event is remembered in the nursery rhyme, "London Bridge Is Falling Down."

According to legend, Olav Haraldsson was waiting in Spain for favorable winds to take him through the Straits of Gibraltar when he dreamed that a man approached him and said, "Return to your home, for you are to be king of Norway for time immemorial." On his way home, Olav spent the winter in Normandy, France, and was converted to Christianity there.

Olav Haraldsson landed in Norway with two shiploads of fighting men in 1015. Within a year he had defeated Olav Tryggvasson's enemies and had himself proclaimed king of Norway. He extended his rule into parts of east Norway, which until then had been under local chieftains, and fought the Danes in the Vik area in the Oslofjord. By 1020, Olav ruled all of Norway as King Olav II.

Olav II also set out to convert Norway, by force when necessary. In this last struggle between the old faith and the new, Christianity finally won. If the farmers refused to accept Christianity at a ting, Olav forced them to change their minds through violence, murder, and fire.

Like Olav I, Olav II's methods won him enemies. The former chieftains, backed by the king of Denmark, attacked Olav II in 1028. Olav fled to Russia but returned in an attempt to win back his kingdom. Finally the opposing forces met in 1030 at a farm called Stiklestad near Trondheim. Outnumbered two to one, Olav was killed and his followers defeated. His body was secretly carried to the city of Trondheim and buried in the sandbank of the River Nid. He was later canonized as Saint Olav.

OTHER CHRISTIAN CHURCHES

Besides the Lutheran Church, several other denominations have adherents in Norway. These include the Pentecostals, Lutheran Free Church members, Methodists, Baptists, Roman Catholics, and Jehovah's Witnesses. Many of these denominations migrated from other European countries.

After the death of Olav II, people began to recall that there had been wondrous signs during the Battle of Stiklestad, and reports of miracles occurring at Olav's grave began to spread throughout the land.

One year after the battle, Olav was declared a saint. Now Norway had its own patron saint, solidifying its ties with the rest of Europe. Olav was acknowledged as a saint throughout Europe and as far away as Constantinople. Churches were built in his honor by the hundreds, not only in Norway but also in Rome and London, where there were at least six built in his name. The day of his death, July 29, became a great religious festival in the north of Europe. Even today, the date is celebrated in Trondheim with reenactments of the battle and other medieval scenes.

Saint Olav had become both a Christian martyr and a champion of national liberty. Down through the ages, his memory lives on as the symbol of a united, independent Norway. He has become the "Eternal King of Norway."

Within five years of his death, two of Olav's former enemies traveled to Russia and brought back his eleven-year-old son Magnus to be king. The foreign rulers fled the country.

After the death of Saint Olav, Christianity came to be accepted as the religion of the country. The old communal beer feasts were incorporated into the observance of holy days. The beer was now blessed and the first cup drunk "in honor of Christ and the Blessed Virgin for good years and peace." However, traces of the old beliefs were slow to disappear. Some forms of nature and ancestor worship lingered on for centuries, and there was no serious attempt to convert the Sami until the sixteenth century.

The Pentecostal movement gained prominence in the early twentieth century in the United States and spread rapidly to all parts of the world. Pentecostal services are enthusiastic and rousing, with an emphasis on music and congregational participation. The Pentecostal movement is attractive to people interested in social reform.

OTHER RELIGIONS

Political instability and economic hardship in nearby lands resulted in a large influx of immigrants into Norway. These immigrants and minority groups brought with them other religions, including Islam, Judaism, Buddhism, and Hinduism. Islam is the largest non-Christian religion in Norway, making up about 2.4 percent of the population in 2013.

INTERNET LINKS

www.theguardian.com/world/2015/feb/04/thor-odin-norse-gods-guide-iceland-temple-vikings-deities
The *Guardian* offers a quick guide to the Norse gods.

kirken.no/nb-NO/church-of-norway/about/brief-history
The Church of Norway site has a brief history of the church.

pilegrimsleden.no/en/about/olav-den-hellige
This site offers an overview of King Olav II (St. Olav).

www.samfunnskunnskap.no/?page_id=360&lang=en
This site gives a basic overview of religion and ethics in Norway.

www.viking-mythology.com
This site has a good deal of information about the Norse gods, with maps and images.

LANGUAGE

A young woman reads a Norwegian newspaper.

9

OVER TIME, HISTORY SHAPES AND changes most languages. Norway's history, in particular, has had a peculiar effect on the Norwegian language—there are two versions of it. In general, however, Norwegian is part of the Germanic family of languages and draws from many European sources. Mountains and fjords historically isolated Norwegian settlements from one another, resulting in numerous dialects existing in Norway. The different dialects are very similar, and all Norwegians can understand each other, regardless of what dialect they speak.

The Sami have their own language, which is part of the Finno-Ugric language family. There are three major Sami dialects in the world, two of which, North Sami and South Sami, are spoken in Norway.

NORWEGIAN

Norwegian and English are related languages because both evolved from a common North Germanic language. English, German, Dutch, and Frisian (a language with variants of it spoken in the Netherlands and Germany) split off long ago, leaving Common Scandinaviar, which was spoken from about 550 to 1050 CE. Common Scandinavian was the parent language of six official, literary languages in Scandinavia—including Danish; Bokmål (BOOK-mawl), which is book Norwegian or Dano-Norwegian; Nynorsk (NEE-noshk), or new Norwegian; Swedish; Faeroese, a West Scandinavian language; and Icelandic—plus a great variety of spoken dialects. Norwegian became a written language in the early twelfth century when the Latin alphabet was introduced in Norway.

Two forms of the Norwegian language, Bokmål and Nynorsk, are officially used. Bokmål developed during Norway's four hundred-year union with Denmark and is mainly spoken in large towns, which were strongly influenced by Danish rule. Spoken Bokmål sounds very different from Danish, but the written form is nearly identical. Created in reaction to Danish rule, Nynorsk dates from the mid-1800s. It combines elements from major rural dialects to produce a more distinctly Norwegian language.

In the twentieth century Norwegian language experts sought to streamline the two official languages into one, called Samnorsk (SAHM-noshk), or common Norwegian. The combined form was intended to simplify communication between urban and rural areas and in the mass media, which now alternate between the two forms. Some Norwegians, however, feel strongly that Bokmål and Nynorsk—as well as the many dialects that influenced them—are part of Norwegian heritage and should not be allowed to vanish. Since 1925, all government officials have been required to answer letters in the language in which they are written. As such, bureaucrats must be competent in both forms of the language. Local school boards decide which form will be used in their elementary school, and the current split is about 20 percent Nynorsk and 80 percent Bokmål. The Samnorsk project was officially abandoned in January 2002.

BOKMÅL VS. NYNORSK

With the many influences on Norwegian throughout the centuries, two approaches to creating a modern Norwegian language have developed. One model, Nynorsk, sought to build a language as close as possible to what

Norwegian might be had it not been under Danish domination for centuries. Ivar Aasen (1813—1869), a linguist and poet, analyzed western Norwegian dialects and formulated a written form for Nynorsk in *Norsk Grammatik* ("Norwegian Grammar"), in 1864, and in *Norsk Ordbog* ("Norwegian Dictionary") in 1873. Since Aasen drew on rural dialects, Nynorsk has great strength in poetic and literary terms describing nature and personal matters. Nynorsk is not the native language of any Norwegian speaker, and it never became the first language of Norway, but it has long had a group of supporters who associate it with a more democratic national consciousness and who see Bokmål as a form of Danish.

Bokmål, earlier called Riksmål (RIKS-mawl), language of the kingdom, used Danish as the base and Norwegianized it through changes in spelling, vocabulary, and pronunciation. Bokmål built on the speech and writings of the educated urban population. In 1856, Knud Knudsen (1812—1895), a linguist and educator, advocated a step-by-step Norwegianization of Danish spelling, a policy followed by such leading writers of the time as Henrik Ibsen. Over the years, Bokmål has retained much of the Danish vocabulary, while accepting some of the Norwegian pronunciation. Bokmål is the language taught abroad as Norwegian today.

After spelling reforms in 1907, 1917, 1938, and 1959, intended to bring the two languages closer, some hoped for the merger of the two languages into Samnorsk. Students reacted in 1960 by burning books translated into Samnorsk. The merged language was never accepted, and today Bokmål and Nynorsk exist side by side.

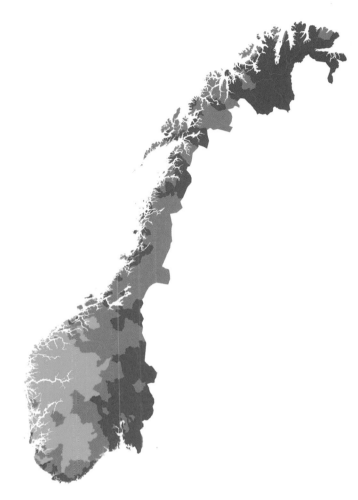

This map shows the official language distribution in Norway's municipalities.

Key:
Blue–Nynorsk
Orange–Bokmål
Gray–neutral

RUNES AND RUNIC WRITING

The oldest written examples of any Germanic languages are the runic inscriptions in Scandinavia. About 3,500 runic inscriptions have been found on objects as diverse as weapons, spear blades, and brooches. The most enduring examples are rune stones—solid stone slabs carved with runes and ornamental designs.

Runes are angular letters that make up the ancient runic alphabet, one of the earliest forms of Germanic writing. Every rune had a special name, and these names are known through the oral traditions recorded in Anglo-Saxon manuscripts. The twenty-four runes of the early runic alphabet were divided into three groups of eight runes each. Each group was called an ætt (eht) in Scandinavia, which is thought to mean a group of eight. Later, the runes were called futhark (FEW-thahrk), which is the word spelled by the first six letters.

The earliest known rune stone dates back to 300 CE. Very little is known about the origin of rune stones, but experts believe they were linked to magic and sorcery, and perhaps religious rituals. It is thought that the common material for runic inscriptions was wood, but none has survived. Surviving rune stones show two runic alphabets: the older, used from the third to the ninth centuries, had twenty-four letters, and the latter had only sixteen letters, a simplification of the earlier alphabet.

Runic inscriptions were often set within a decorated snake or dragon coil. Occasionally other ornamental designs were used as well. Stone engravers sometimes took it upon themselves to include additional information to the commissioned text. Much of our information about the political, economic, and cultural conditions of those times comes from these rune stones. The stones also tell of Viking journeys as far away as Byzantium and Baghdad, as many were memorials to someone who died on the journeys. It is from the pictures on these stones that we know Old Norse legends of Sigurd, the dragon slayer, and Thor, the thunder god.

THE SAMI LANGUAGES

The Sami language is not Germanic, as Norwegian is, but is part of the Finno-Ugric language family, related to Finnish and Hungarian. Sami speakers are divided into three main dialect groups: North Sami, mostly spoken in northern Norway, Finland, and Sweden; East Sami, which includes Inari and Skolt in Eastern Finland and Kola Sami from the Kola Peninsula of Russia; and the least common, South Sami, still represented by a few scattered speakers from central Norway to north-central Sweden. At least two versions of Sami are now extinct, with the last known speaker of Akkala Sami having died in 2003. Each of these dialect groups has various subgroups. Sami dialects are so different from one another that a member of one dialect group cannot understand a member of another. When Norwegian Sami of different dialect groups meet, they communicate in Norwegian.

North Sami has a literary tradition that began with the seventeenth-century Swedish Sami Bible and other religious translations. In the mid-twentieth century, elementary schools that used Sami as the language of instruction were found in many larger North Sami communities. The Sami in Norway use a special system of writing that was created to accommodate a wide range of variations in dialects.

The vocabulary of the Sami does not include words for war, farming, or other things that are unfamiliar to them. When it comes to nature, though, they are not lacking: they have about three hundred words for describing snow and ice!

INTERNET LINKS

www.omniglot.com/writing/norwegian.htm
Omniglot gives a good introduction to Norwegian with recorded samples in both Nynorsk and Bokmål.

www.omniglot.com/writing/saami.htm
All of the Sami languages are discussed on this site, with links to different versions.

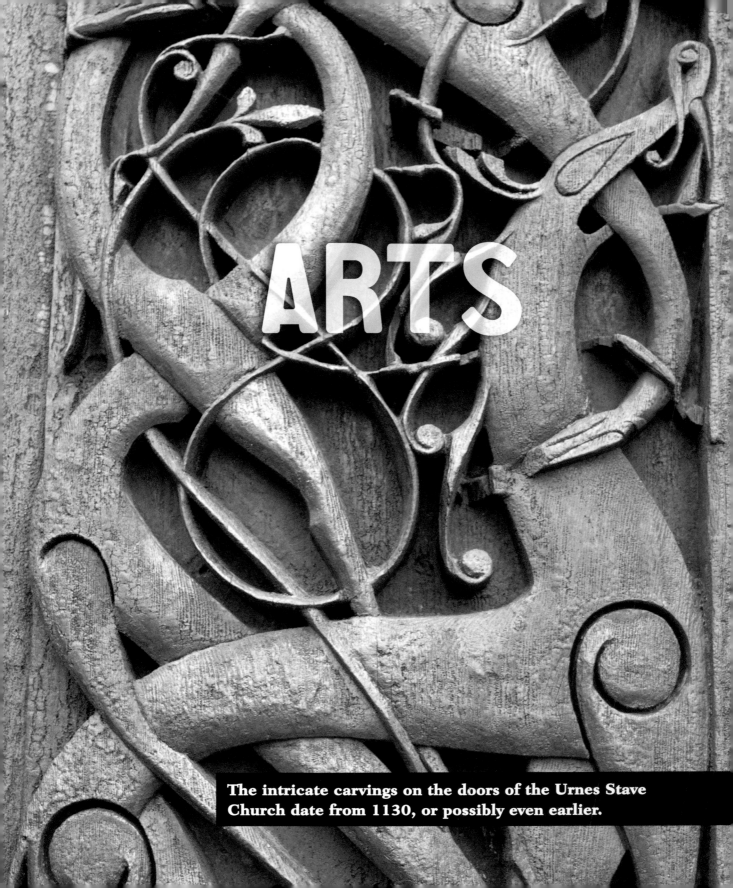

ARTS

The intricate carvings on the doors of the Urnes Stave Church date from 1130, or possibly even earlier.

10

FROM THE VIKING CRAFTSMEN AND storytellers to the rockers in the annual Norwegian Wood Rock Festival in Oslo, Norway has a strong arts tradition. The arts really blossomed here beginning in the nineteenth century. Prior to that, Vikings artists aside, most Norwegians imported or copied art from Europe. Today, Norway has a vibrant arts scene, combining the best of the old with the newest of the new.

"For as long as I can remember I have suffered from a deep feeling of anxiety which I have tried to express in my art."
—Edvard Munch (1863-1944), Norwegian artist

VIKING ART

The Vikings (800—1050 CE) are best remembered as sea-going warriors, murderers, and plunderers, and that reputation is well deserved. However, these rugged Scandinavian people also created some beautiful objects. Among the oldest artworks in Norway are the complex carvings made by Viking artisans to decorate ships, buildings, wagons, sleighs, swords, and many other objects. They also crafted gold jewelry. Viking design styles usually involved intricate, looping, interwoven elements, and sometimes animals and monstrous beasts. Many of those artifacts survive to this day, especially the metalwork. The Viking Ship Museum in Oslo holds many such relics, including the world's two best-preserved wooden Viking ships built in the ninth century.

The Vikings were also great poets and storytellers. Intricate skaldic verse (Old Norse heroic poetry) was passed on orally for generations until it was written down centuries later.

PAINTING

In the nineteenth century, paintings of Norwegian landscapes and scenes of daily life replaced the previous motifs of Christian and Viking themes. Johan Christian Dahl (1788—1857) was at the forefront of the development of a Norwegian style of painting. Dahl introduced the mountain as a symbol that would recur in the works of later artists and writers. He taught in Dresden, Germany.

EDVARD MUNCH Norway's best-known artist is Edvard Munch (1863—1944). Munch's ability to portray the trauma of modern psychic life through distortion of colors and forms made him one of the most influential modern artists.

Munch, who came from an old Norwegian professional family, was greatly affected by the deaths of his mother when he was five years old and his eldest sister when he was fourteen. Many critics feel that Munch's childhood explains the melancholy in his paintings. His better-known works include *The Sick Child, Ashes, Death in the Room, Jealousy,* and *Summer Night.* Munch gave his works to the city of Oslo, where some of them are now housed at the Munch Museum.

SCULPTURE

The first Norwegian sculptor to win international fame, Gustav Vigeland (1869—1943), has an entire park in Oslo dedicated to him. Vigeland Museum, which has Vigeland's ashes and many of his works, is also located in Vigeland Park. In the 1920s the municipality of Oslo offered Vigeland this building for his studio and residence. In return, he donated all his works to the city.

Vigeland Park was designed by Vigeland himself. The park exhibits many of his best works, whose main theme is the various phases of human life,

THE SCREAM

Edvard Munch's best-known work, which he called The Scream of Nature, *but which has come to be called* Skrik *("The Scream"), is actually a series of four versions of the same scene that he made over several years—two rendered in tempera paints, and two in pastels. In addition, he made numerous black and white lithograph prints of the same image. In his diary, Munch described the inspiration for the scene:*

"One evening I was walking along a path, the city was on one side and the fjord below. I felt tired and ill. I stopped and looked out over the fjord—the sun was setting, and the clouds turning blood red. I sensed a scream passing through nature; it seemed to me that I heard the scream. I painted this picture, painted the clouds as actual blood. The color shrieked. This became The Scream.*"*

The iconic image has since been copied, referenced, and parodied in all forms of popular culture, including an episode of The Simpsons.

In 1994, on Opening Day of the 1994 Winter Olympics in Lillehammer, Norway, two men broke into the National Gallery in Oslo and stole its version of The Scream. *In its place, they left a note reading, "Thanks for the poor security." The painting was recovered later that year. In August 2004, the other painted version was stolen from the Munch Museum in Oslo, along with another Munch painting,* Madonna. *The Munch Museum was subsequently closed in order to revamp and beef up its security. In 2006, Norwegian police announced that they recovered both* The Scream *and* Madonna, *but would not reveal the details of the operation. Six suspects went on trial and three were convicted for the roles they had played in the theft. In 2008, after repairs were made to the stolen and somewhat damaged artworks, they were again put on exhibit.*

Meanwhile, in 2012, one of the pastel versions of The Scream *was sold at auction for a record price of nearly $120 million.*

from infancy to old age. Many of his sculptures represent scenes from everyday life. In *Angry Boy*, Vigeland immortalized a young boy throwing a tantrum. The work that most people see as the park's main masterpiece is *The Monolith*, a sculpture 55 feet (17 m) tall, representing 121 humans struggling toward a summit. Vigeland Park, which also features a sculpted self-portrait of Vigeland, draws over one million visitors a year.

MUSIC

Norway has a long tradition of music that includes folk songs, fiddling, and brass bands. It even has a fiddle to call its own. The *Hardingfele*, or "Hardanger fiddle," is similar to a violin but has eight or nine strings. Four strings are the main strings, as on a violin, but the Hardanger fiddle also has additional understrings which resonate when the top four are played. This creates a distinctive sound that is used in traditional Norwegian folk and dance music.

Just about every school has a marching band, which is where many of Norway's jazz musicians got their start. In fact, the country has become a world-class center of jazz and blues, two quintessentially American forms, which Norwegian musicians have embraced and turned into distinctly Norwegian musical styles. Hip hop, too, is popular in Norway, as is pop and rock, of course.

The indie folk-pop duo called Kings of Convenience, from Bergen, have had some success in the United States and Europe. They are known for their sophisticated harmonies, calming voices, and serene acoustic melodies. Their most recent album, *Declaration of Dependence* (2009), like their previous albums, is recorded in English.

Modern composer Arne Nordheim (1931—2010) took Norwegian classical music by storm two generations after Grieg's death. He produced experimental works, often combining orchestral music with taped electronically processed acoustic sounds. From 1982 until his death in 2010, Nordheim and his wife had lived in Grotten, the Norwegian government's residence for the leading artistic figure of the day, next to Oslo's royal palace.

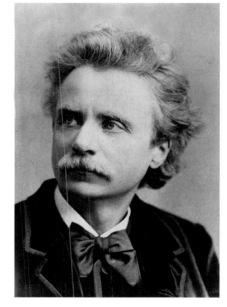

Norway's most famous composer—and indeed one of Norway's greatest and most beloved historical figures—is Edvard Grieg (1843–1907). Grieg did not write symphonies, but he did take on large projects. He is most acclaimed for his Peer Gynt Suite, the music for Henrik Ibsen's 1867 play, Peer Gynt, which is based on a Norwegian fairytale. The suites include the famous pieces, "In the Hall of the Mountain King" and "Morning Mood," which, because they are frequently heard in popular culture, are familiar to many people who don't even realize the origins of the music. Both pieces and others from the Peer Gynt Suite are so iconic today as to be almost synonymous with Norway itself.

Grieg is also known for his piano sonatas, ten volumes of lyrical pieces inspired by the poems of Henrik Ibsen and Arne Garborg. Grieg, who also wrote Norwegian folk songs and music for Norwegian dances, is equally well known in Norway for a little rubber frog that he kept in his pocket. It is believed that by rubbing its rough-textured back before a concert he calmed his nerves. The frog is part of the permanent Grieg exhibit at the composer's home.

LITERATURE

Norwegian Vikings who settled in Iceland orally passed on their beliefs, history, and myths through stories. These were written down in the thirteenth-century Eddas, books that tell of the various mythical gods and heroes of Scandinavia.

The first important writer of the modern period was Henrik Wergeland (1808—1845). He wrote love and nature poems and numerous essays. He established a free personal lending library. A devout nationalist, Wergeland called upon Norwegians to free themselves of Danish influence, and he set up a school in his own home where he taught Norwegian. He set the pattern for creative writers to be public advocates for democracy and freedom.

Wergeland's sister Camilla Collett (1813—1895) wrote Norway's first feminist novel, *The Governor's Daughter*—the first part published in 1854 and the second in 1855—decrying the position of women forced into marriage. Collett inspired other female writers, including Amalie Skram (1847—1905) who, in her novels *Constance Ring* and *Betrayed*, continued Collett's theme of disastrous marriages.

Around the beginning of the twentieth century, Norwegian writers focused on the struggles of the individual. Many twentieth-century novels explore social problems and feature protagonists who reject modern society. In 1920 Knut Hamsun (1859—1952), best known for his novels *Hunger* and *Growth of the Sun*, was awarded the Nobel Prize in literature.

Norwegian literature thrived throughout the century, though only a few writers achieved international fame. Poet and novelist Tarjei Vesaas (1897—1970) is widely considered to be one of Norway's greatest writers of the twentieth century. His works are written in Nynorsk and focus on rural lives and the Norwegian natural landscape. His most famous book is *The Ice Palace*, first published in 1963.

Current authors who have attracted global attention include the prolific crime writer Jo Nesbø (b. 1960); Per Petterson (b. 1952), whose novel *Out Stealing Horses* was named one of the Ten Best Books of the Year by the *New York Times Book Review* in 2007; and Karl Ove Knausgård (b. 1968), whose six autobiographical novels in the controversial series called *My Struggle* have made him a household name in Norway. Journalist and nonfiction writer Åsne Seierstad (b. 1970) is best known for her accounts of life in war zones. *The Bookseller of Kabul* (2002) was a best seller. Her newest book, *One of Us: The Story of a Massacre in Norway—and Its Aftermath* (2015) is about the 2011 mass murder on Utoya. This highly acclaimed book was named a Best Book of the Year by *The New York Times Book Review* and many other notable US media sources.

HENRIK IBSEN *The work of Henrik Ibsen (1828–1906) revolutionized theater. His plays aroused enormous criticism, but people flocked to see them. James Joyce, the great Irish writer, was so enamored of Ibsen's plays that he taught himself Norwegian in order to study them. A strong supporter of women's rights, Ibsen is known for creating many great female characters, such as Nora in* A Doll's House, *which is about women's liberation and the hypocrisy of marriage.*

Ibsen's major plays are set in Norway, with a recognizably Norwegian landscape, but his characters and themes have universal significance. Ibsen portrayed people as they are; his characters struggle with problems that society of their time was afraid to mention, such as marital discord and illegitimacy. Over the course of fifty years, Ibsen published twenty-five plays and a volume of poetry. His plays are still regularly performed today.

SIGRID UNDSET, THE NOBEL LAUREATE *In 1928 another Norwegian writer, Sigrid Undset (1882–1949), was awarded the Nobel Prize in literature for her long historical novel* Kristin Lavransdatter, *set in thirteenth-century Norway. Undset, considered Norway's greatest woman writer, was taught the Old Norse sagas and Scandinavian folk songs at an early age by her archaeologist father. Undset's novels provide insight into women's lives not found elsewhere in Norwegian fiction. Her early novels centered on the lives of ordinary working women and how they dealt with conflicts between personal needs and ambitions and family responsibilities.*

During the 1930s, Undset wrote vehemently against the rise of Nazism in Germany, which put her on the Nazis' most-wanted list. When the Nazis occupied Norway, Undset escaped to Sweden, then made her way across Siberia to Japan, and then to the United States. She spent the war years actively working for the Norwegian government in exile. After the war, she returned to her home in Lillehammer and died four years later.

DRAMA

By European standards, Norway's theater traditions are very young. Professional theater began only in 1827, when Swedish Johan Peter Strømberg opened his theater in Oslo. Norway's oldest existing theater is the National Stage in Bergen, which was opened in 1876.

Henrik Ibsen, Norway's most famous playwright, well-known all over the world for plays such as *Peer Gynt* and *A Doll's House*, is acknowledged as the father of modern Norwegian drama. Norway also had another prominent playwright, Nordahl Grieg, who wrote plays that deal with the human psyche and question one's inner self.

The National Traveling Theater, or Riksteatret (riks-teh-AH-ter-eht), was founded in 1948, using the Swedish Riksteatret as its model. The Riksteatret takes professional drama all over Norway, to towns and villages that would otherwise be deprived as they are too small to support their own theater companies. It is the equivalent of the circus coming to town, and no one who can help it will miss a performance of the Riksteatret.

Permanent theaters are awarded grants by government, county, and local authorities that cover almost 90 percent of their operating expenses.

STAVKIRKER ARCHITECTURE

Norway's rich tradition in wood carving is documented in stories from the medieval period when carpentry was a craft entrusted only to men of rank. When Norway was converted to Christianity, Norwegians developed their own form of religious architecture in the *stavkirker* (stahv-KHEER-ker), or stave churches, which are thought to be quintessentially Norwegian. Norway had over one thousand of these wooden churches in the medieval period. Only about thirty remain intact.

No nails were used in the construction of stave churches. Norwegian pine wood was measured and cut precise lengths to form planks, columns and beams, then pieced together. Stave churches were also traditionally raised above ground level to preserve the wooden structure from rotting. The stave churches retained Viking design elements and also displayed Christian

ROSEMALING, THE DECORATIVE FOLK PAINTING OF NORWAY

Rosemaling, the decorative folk painting of Norway, is a distinctive folk art that incorporates flowery ornamentation, scrollwork, and flowing patterns. It originated in the rural lowland areas of eastern Norway around 1750 and was popular there for about a century. As rural painters began copying the style, regional differences emerged, with the Telemark, Hallingal, and Rogaland styles becoming the main forms. Artisans used colorful rosemaling designs to decorate household objects, furniture, walls, and even clothing. While most designs feature stylized flowers, leaves, and vines, in some cases alphabet letters and figures of people are included. One thing that is almost never seen in rosemaling is a straight line.

When Norwegian emigrants traveled to America in the nineteenth century, they often carried their belongings in beautifully rosemaled trunks. These pretty objects created new interest in the folk art and launched revival of rosemaling in the United States. Today, rosemaling is taught in many places in the United States, especially those with large Norwegian communities. The Vesterheim Norwegian-American Museum in Decorah, Iowa, is known for its large collection of both Norwegian and American rosemaled objects. It offers classes and olds an annual national rosemaling competition.

influences from other parts of Europe. These churches were small, dark, and plain, without pews or pulpits. The most distinctive art works could be found at the doorframe where animals and intertwining lines, similar to Viking wood carvings, decorated the doors, especially the large west doors that served as the main entrance.

FOLK DRESS The only district where folk dress is still worn daily as well as for holidays is Samiland. In the winter the Sami who inhabit the area that used to be called Lappland wear fur on their heads and bodies, right to their feet, but in the summer they wear their most colorful traditional clothing. This has fabric patterned with delicate embroidery around the throat and shoulders. Samis often wear beautiful belts woven in bright colors.

THE JOIK An old Sami form of musical expression is the joik (yoy-IK), a type of yodeling. Traditionally, the joik imitates animals, such as the wolf, reindeer, or long-tailed duck. A joik can also tell an ancient Sami myth or serve as a commentary on current events. The most popular forms of joik are character sketches of individuals that can be changed as the person changes. A Sami does not write his or her own joik, and once one is written about a person, it is customary to regard it as belonging to that person. The memory of deceased persons is kept alive by reciting their joik.

In traditional religious ceremonies the joik was used to help the shaman—a religious figure who performs a priestlike role—enter a trance while beating a drum. During the Norwegianization process, the joik and drumming were outlawed. Today, Sami revivalization has evoked a renewed interest in the joik tradition, and it has acquired value as an important cultural symbol. In recent years one joik made it to the top of the Norwegian hit parade.

theculturetrip.com/europe/norway/articles/norway-s-best-artists-and-where-to-find-them
This article highlights some of Norway's finest contemporary artists.

www.edvardmunch.org
This site contains a biography, analysis, and gallery of Munch's paintings.

griegmuseum.no/en
The Grieg Museum site includes a biography, a timeline, and a gallery about the life and works of Edvard Grieg.

www.popspotsnyc.com/The_Scream
The writer of PopSpots tells a fascinating story of discovering the real-life site of Munch's *The Scream* in Oslo.

whc.unesco.org/en/list/58
The Urnes Stave Church in Sognefjord is the subject of this entry on the UNESCO World Heritage site.

vesterheim.org
The National Norwegian American Museum and Heritage Center presents a downloadable booklet about rosemaling.

www.visitnorway.com/things-to-do/art-culture
This site offers information about a wide range of arts and cultural events and destinations.

LEISURE

A family on cross-country skis stops to admire the view.

11

W ITH ALL ITS MOUNTAINOUS, snowy terrain, it's no wonder Norway is nearly synonymous with skiing. This manner of traversing snowy landscapes is not a recent invention. A four thousand-year-old rock carving in Nordland near the Arctic Circle shows a person on two skis. Skis about 2,300 years old have been found preserved in bogs. Old Norse mythology had both a ski god, Ull, and a ski goddess, Skade.

A NATION OF SKIERS

Almost every Norwegian owns a pair of skis. Norwegians take their first skiing lessons at age two or three. Schoolchildren look forward to ski days and ski vacations, and adults often go off on ski runs to unwind after a hard day at work. After dusk, adults ski the many miles of lighted trails through woods wearing a cap with a light, similar to a miner's cap. Those feeling deprived during the summer often pack their skis and make their way to the glaciers of Jotunheimen National Park.

Norway is known as the home of modern skiing. Sondre Norheim (1825—1897), a poor farmer from Morgedal in the Telemark region, devised a ski that was narrower in the middle and had stiff bindings around the heel. This was called the Telemark ski, and it enabled

Liv Arnesen, a forty-one-year-old Norwegian, became the first woman to reach the South Pole alone when she arrived there on Christmas Day, 1994, after skiing 746 miles (1,200 km) in fifty days.

Norheim to execute jumps and turns without losing his skis, earning him the title of "father of modern skiing."

Norheim and some other ski enthusiasts soon became known for their daring feats. They entered competitions where they could demonstrate their techniques. Norheim was fifty when he retired from competitions, but he taught his techniques to children. Later, he went to the United States, where others from Telemark had introduced skiing.

The first recorded skiing competitions with prizes in Norway date from 1866. By 1903, foreigners were taking part in the annual competitions. With the popularity of skiing as a sport instead of simply as a form of transportation, hotels that previously closed for the winter discovered they could now stay open all year round. In 1924 the first Winter Olympics were held in Chamonix, France, with Norwegians taking the top four spots in the 31-mile (50 km) race.

THE GREAT OUTDOORS

Skiing isn't the only sport that Norwegians love. Soccer is very popular, as it is in most other parts of the world. Boating, fishing, rowing, swimming, hiking, and cycling are also favorite activities.

Norway's grand and beautiful wilderness areas, which have inspired artists and musicians, are accessible to everyone in Norway. Norwegians spend much of their free time hiking, skiing, fishing, cycling, and mountain climbing. In fact, the reluctance of Oslo residents to leave the city—it lies in the middle of the Nordmarka forest area—because they are so fond of walks through the woods is referred to as the "Nordmarka syndrome." The Norwegian Mountain Touring Association, the oldest organization of its kind in the world, marks trails and rents out cabins for overnight accommodation to help hikers.

The right of access to uncultivated areas is very important in Norway. Fortunately, along with free access, most Norwegians are conscious of their obligations. They know they may not walk in newly planted forest; break off, cut, or in any way damage plants; disturb animals and birds, including their nests and young; or trample fields and meadows.

NORWAY AND THE OLYMPICS

Norway has twice hosted the Winter Olympic Games—the 1952 Games in Oslo, and the 1994 Games in Lillehammer. The first time, in Oslo, the home country advantage paid off, with Norway ranking number 1. At Lillehammer, which was a much larger competition, Norway won the most medals, but came in second to Russia in the ranking because the Russians won eleven gold medals to Norway's ten.

Norway bid for the 2018 Olympics but lost to PyeongChang, South Korea. Norway tried again for the 2022 Olympics, but ended up withdrawing its bid, as did Stockholm, Sweden; Lviv, Ukraine; and Krakow, Poland. The expense of hosting the games as well as disagreements with the International Olympic Committee (IOC) made Norway think twice. However, the country will certainly participate in those Olympic Games in any event.

In the 2014 Winter Olympics in Sochi, Russia, Norway won twenty-six medals, including eleven gold. Marit Bjørgen (b. 1980) won three gold, making her one of the three most medaled women in Winter Olympic history—and of those three, the one with the most gold medals. Of the men, Ole Einar Bjørndalen (b. 1974), nicknamed "the King of Biathlon," won two gold medals in his sport. He is the most medaled athlete in the history of the Winter Olympics.

Ole Einar Bjørndalen

ICE SKATING

The first speed-skating contest in Norway was held on the ice in a fjord near Oslo's Akershus Fortress in 1885. In the 1950s speed-skating champions were national heroes. Since then, interest in the sport has diminished, although in 1991 Norway gained a new national hero in Johan Koss, who made sports history when he broke three world records during the world speed-skating championships in the Netherlands, followed by winning a gold medal at the 1994 Winter Olympics.

In figure skating, Sonja Henie, Norway's darling of the 1920s, brought fame to Norway as the world's figure-skating champion at age fifteen. She retained the title for ten years and won the Olympic gold medal three times. She also starred in many popular Hollywood movies during the late 1930s and early 1940s.

WOMEN IN SPORTS

Although Norwegian women today win many of the top spots in international sporting events such as marathons, handball, and soccer, it has been only recently that female athletes were fully accepted in Norway. In 1888 Lillehammer sponsored the world's first ski races for women, but it is only since the 1960s that Norwegian women have been taken seriously in cross-country skiing competitions.

The acceptance of sportswomen in Norway is attributed to Grete Waitz (b. 1953), who won the New York marathon in nine out of ten races between 1978 and 1988. She started an organized run through the streets of Oslo in 1982, and it has since become an annual event.

EXPLORERS

Harking back to the traditional occupation of their Viking ancestors as daring explorers who set sail for parts unknown, several Norwegians have attempted grueling expeditions to far reaches of the earth. They include Fridtjof Nansen, Otto Sverdrup, Roald Amundsen, Thor Heyerdahl, Ragnar Thorseth, and, most recently, Liv Arnesen.

FRIDTJOF NANSEN Before he became a delegate to the League of Nations, Fridtjof Nansen (1861—1930) was a well-known scientist. To prove his hypothesis that the Arctic current flowed from Siberia toward the North Pole and then down to Greenland, Nansen designed a boat, the *Fram*, that would not break apart under the enormous pressure of ice. In July 1893, along with thirteen crew members, he headed east from Vardø in the far northeast of Norway.

Grete Waitz waves to the crowd in 1983 after winning a gold medal for the marathon event at the Olympic Games in Helsinki, Finland.

This engraving illustrates the *Fram* frozen into the Arctic ice.

Off the northeast coast of Siberia, the *Fram* was frozen into the ice pack. With knowledge gained from years of study, Nansen knew the boat would not pass over the North Pole. With a companion, three light sleds, twenty-eight dogs, three kayaks, and food for one hundred days, he set out in March 1895 for the North Pole.

By early April, Nansen realized they would not make it to the North Pole, although he had gone farther than any previous explorer. They then attempted to journey to Franz Joseph Land, 400 miles (640 km) to the southwest. In August they reached an uninhabited island north of Franz Joseph Land. As winter was closing in, they dug a three-foot hollow, made a roof of walrus skins, and sat out the nine-month winter.

In June 1896 they made it to one of the southern islands, where they encountered the English explorer Frederick Jackson, who had been commissioned to find an overland route to the North Pole. Nansen returned to Norway on Jackson's ship to a hero's welcome. A week later the *Fram* arrived in Norway, having drifted from Siberia to Svalbard, proving Nansen's theory true.

OTTOS VERDRUP The captain of the *Fram* for Nansen's drift expedition, Otto Sverdrup (1854—1930), took the *Fram* on a second expedition to the Arctic islands north of Canada and spent four years charting unexplored territory. Between 1910 and 1920, he led other polar expeditions. His maps were a valuable resource for explorers who came after him.

ROALD AMUNDSEN Like Fridtjof Nansen, Roald Amundsen (1872—1928) was a professional expeditioner who knew that courage had to

PLANTING THE NORWEGIAN FLAG AT THE SOUTH POLE

After months of preparation, Roald Amundsen was just about to set out in Nansen's Fram for the North Pole when news that American Robert Peary had reached it reverberated around the world. Amundsen immediately changed his course for Antarctica and the South Pole, determined to reach it ahead of the British expedition headed by Robert Scott.

At the Bay of Whales in the Ross Sea, Amundsen set out overland with four men and fifty-two dogs. One of the four men was Olav Bjaaland, a skiing champion from Morgedal, who was given the task of making sure the skis and sleds were in top condition all the time. On December 14, 1911, the Norwegian group reached the South Pole and planted the Norwegian flag on King Haakon VII's Plateau. This was the expedition that

made Roald Amundsen a household name around the world. Five weeks later, Robert Scott arrived at the pole to find the Norwegian flag and Amundsen's tent.

Amundsen died in 1928 while attempting to rescue Umberto Nobile, an explorer whose airship had crashed while attempting to fly over the North Pole. At a memorial service for Amundsen, who was buried in the Arctic, Fridtjof Nansen said that Amundsen had "returned to the expanses of the Arctic Ocean, where his life's work lay."

be supplemented with careful planning. He realized that success for an Arctic expedition meant combining the roles of scientist and navigator. In preparation, he not only trained physically by playing soccer, skiing, and sleeping with the window open in the winter, but also studied navigation and the theories of magnetism. Amundsen wanted to be the first to navigate the so-called Northwest Passage.

Thor Heyerdahl and his crewmates on board the *Kon-Tiki* in 1947.

In the previous four hundred years, fifty or sixty expeditions had been launched without success. In 1903, with a crew of six, Amundsen set out to find and navigate the Northwest Passage in a thirty-one-year-old small herring boat. He was convinced the smallness of his vessel and patience would get him farther than the others, who had used much larger boats.

Amundsen was right. He got through the entire Northwest Passage, including a shallow island-dotted strait never before navigated. He wrote later that "it was just like sailing through an uncleared field." If he had been in a larger boat, he would not have succeeded.

THOR HEYERDAHL Perhaps the best-known explorer of the twentieth century, Thor Heyerdahl (1914—2000) did not follow in the footsteps of Nansen or Amundsen by exploring unchartered territories. Anthropology was his interest.

As a zoology and geography student, he traveled in 1937 to Polynesia to conduct research on animal life in the valleys of the island of Fatu-Hiva. Accepting anthropological theories that ancestors of the Polynesians had sailed there from Asia, Heyerdahl noticed something different that contradicted the theories: the people had much in common with South Americans in food, statues, and myths.

To prove the scientists who argued that South Americans could not have reached Polynesia in their primitive vessels wrong, Heyerdahl launched his famous *Kon Tiki* expedition. In 1947, he built a raft in the style of the Incas—a log raft held together by ropes and wooden pegs—and set out from Peru with five companions. In 101 days, having sailed 5,000 miles (8,045 km) across the Pacific Ocean on the *Kon-Tiki*, he reached the Raroia Atoll in Polynesia.

He did not prove that the Polynesians' ancestors came from South America, but Heyerdahl showed that it might have been possible.

Heyerdahl later made many other voyages in replicas of prehistoric boats. He traveled on papyrus reed boats, named *Ra I* and *Ra II*, from North Africa to the Caribbean in 1969 and 1970. In 1978, he sailed from the Middle East to East Asia and back to Africa in an Iraqi reed boat. All of Heyerdahl's voyages attempted to show the links between major early civilizations. Heyerdahl believed that the world's oceans have served as highways for humankind since the first boats were built.

In 2011, the Thor Heyerdahl Archives, including his photographic collection, diaries, private letters, expedition plans, articles, newspaper clippings, original book, and article manuscripts, were added to UNESCO's "Memory of the World" Register. This international initiative, launched by UNESCO in 1992, is meant to "safeguard the documentary heritage of humanity against collective amnesia, neglect, the ravages of time and climatic conditions, and willful and deliberate destruction."

INTERNET LINKS

ngm.nationalgeographic.com/2009/01/nansen/sides-text
"1,000 Days in the Ice," a feature about Fritjof Nansen, includes a photo gallery.

www.pbs.org/wgbh/amex/ice/peopleevents/pandeAMEX87.html
A profile of Roald Amundsen is part of the PBS site "Alone on the Ice."

www.smithsonianmag.com/history/kon-tiki-sails-again-5404357
"Kon Tiki Sails Again" tells the story of Thor Heyerdahl and the *Kon-Tiki* expedition in the light of a new movie, released in 2013.

www.visitnorway.com/hotels-more/ski-resorts
This travel site gives information about Norway's ski resorts.

FESTIVALS

A couple dresses in traditional clothing for Norwegian Constitution Day on May 17, 2014.

12

NORWEGIANS WORK HARD IN THE course of the year, so they really let their hair down and celebrate on festival days. The streets are filled with people, and in the cities and towns it looks like one big party. Summer time, in particular, is filled with music, arts, film, and food festivals. Outdoor rock, jazz, and pop music concerts are big, and Norwegians are particularly well known for metal, indie, and electronica bands and performers.

Being a predominantly Christian nation, Norway naturally celebrates the holidays of the church calendar, such as Christmas, Easter, and various saints' days. But some of the country's festive traditions, such as Midsummer's Day, harken back to pre-Christian times. Norwegians also celebrate national and local festivals, such as their Constitution Day and *russ* (rewss) celebrations.

EASTER

Easter celebrations are less a religious occasion in Norway than a rejoicing in the lengthening of the days, a sign that summer is not too far away. In the north, the Sami gather to celebrate weddings,

NATIONAL HOLIDAYS IN NORWAY

January 1 . . . . *New Year's Day*

March/April . . . . . *Holy Thursday through Easter Monday*

May 1 . . . . *Labor Day*

May/June . . . . *Ascension Day (forty days after Easter)*

May/June . . . . *Whitsunday/Whitmonday (Pentecost; seventh Sunday after Easter)*

May 17 . . . . *Constitution Day*

December 25 . . . . . *Christmas Day*

December 26 . . . . . *Boxing Day*

confirmations, and baptisms, and all Norwegians who live north of the Arctic Circle celebrate the return of the sun after weeks of darkness.

Although many Norwegians spend the five-day Easter break with family and close friends, Easter is also a time for celebrating solitude and independence and communing with nature. Many Norwegians take off on solitary journeys and travel up into the mountains to do just that. A popular Easter joke tells of a Norwegian professor who, when asked how he had enjoyed his Easter holiday in the mountains, replied, "It was a total failure. I met somebody."

CONSTITUTION DAY

Constitution Day is the Norwegian equivalent of the Fourth of July celebrations in the United States. It falls on May 17, the anniversary of the day in 1814 when Norway's elected National Assembly issued a constitution that declared an end to the four-hundred-year union with Denmark.

Constitution Day has been celebrated in various ways over the decades. After independence in 1905, parades emphasized nationhood. During the Nazi occupation of World War II, Constitution Day celebrations were forbidden. In the decades since World War II, parades have emphasized democratic rights, freedom of the press, and constitutional government.

CHILDREN'S DAY

May 17 has also become Children's Day in Norway, and thousands of schoolchildren participate in processions with their school bands in cities, towns, and villages all over the country. The Oslo parade ends at the Royal Palace, where the royal family waves to the children from a balcony.

The day is marked by firecrackers set off at dawn, between 4 and 5 a.m. High school graduates drive around in cars decorated with flowers and branches, wearing their graduation suits. For them, Constitution Day marks the beginning of a three-week celebration of the end of high school.

A children's parade marches on Constitution Day.

RUSS CELEBRATIONS

High school graduates celebrate their graduation in a unique style, wearing their russ costumes and engaging in a three-week-long celebration. The term *russ* originated from a Latin word that refers to those who were sent to the university to study. Most russ are so-called *rødrusser* (red russ), graduates in the arts and the sciences, while *blåruss* (blue russ) are those who graduated in business, and *svartruss* (black russ) is for those who focused on vocational subjects.

Russ students are allowed many liberties. They are permitted to make as much noise as they wish, early in the morning, late at night, or all day. They can spray silly jingles about their teachers on the pavements with washable paint, or serenade teachers in the early hours of the morning. They can have as much fun as they wish, provided they do not engage in acts of vandalism that destroy property or harm anyone.

Teachers are not the only targets of russ students. Neighbors may have a rude, but never insulting, jingle about them sprayed on the pavement in front of their house. They will be embarrassed by it, but it is all permitted and accepted in a spirit of fun.

MIDSUMMER'S DAY

A Midsummer's Eve bonfire in Balestrand celebrates the kickoff to summer.

Midsummer, or the summer solstice, is the longest day of the year. (Centuries ago in Europe, spring wasn't considered a separate season, and summer began on the spring equinox. That's why "midsummer" is actually the day of the summer solstice, now the first day of summer.) Early Vikings often held their assemblies on Midsummer's Day, which was also allegedly the annual meeting day for witches. The feast of the bonfires on the summer solstice is one of the oldest celebrations in northern Europe. In Christian times, the day was renamed Saint John's Eve, in honor of John the Baptist. Today heaps of wood are collected for days beforehand. On Midsummer's Eve, huge bonfires are lit, and the crowd drinks, eats, and dances all night long.

CHRISTMAS

Jul (yewl), or Christmas, is more than just one day—it's a season. In fact, the word "jul" was the name of a month in the old Germanic calendar, and is still thought of as a period of time, typically mid-November to mid-January. It's a busy time for churches, which hold special Advent services. It's busy as well for households—traditionally, all the wood must be cut, cakes baked, food prepared, and beer brewed by December 21, Saint Thomas's Day.

On Christmas Eve, families sit down to a traditional Christmas dinner. In northern and western Norway, this is likely to be *pinnekjøtt* (PINE-shuht). Meaning "twig meat," it is a dish of lamb ribs, so named because a rack of birch twigs is placed in the bottom of the pan used to steam the ribs. In the eastern part of the country, *ribbe*, a pork rib roast, is often served with dumplings. In southern Norway, cod and lutefisk are traditional Jul dishes. According to custom, seven kinds of pastry are served, with *pepperkaker* (gingerbread), *krumkake* (curved waffle cookies), and *kringla* (pretzel-shaped cookies) being especially beloved. Gløgg, descended from the Viking drink mead, is a favorite Christmas drink. Wine or juice is mulled with raisins, ginger, cardamom, cinnamon, and other spices, and served warm. After the meal the family gathers around the Christmas tree singing traditional carols. Children happily anticipate a visit from Julenisse (traditionally the Christmas elf; today, Santa Claus). Gifts are exchanged and opened and celebrations last for twenty days, until Saint Knut's Day, on January 13.

INTERNET LINKS

www.roughguides.com/destinations/europe/norway/festivals-events
This travel site lists festivals and events as well as holidays.

www.timeanddate.com/holidays/norway
This site lists the dates for both formal and informal holidays in Norway with links to explanations.

FOOD

NYKOKTE FJORDREKER 1/2 Kg Kr. 150

Sjøkre 420,- pr kg

Fresh seafood on ice is displayed at a Bergen fish market.

13

WHAT IS NORWAY'S FAVORITE food? People who know a bit about Norwegian cuisine might guess pickled herring or smoked salmon, and they wouldn't necessarily be wrong. The surprising answer, however, just might be pizza. Norwegians actually eat more pizza, per person per year, than Americans do! Norwegians jokingly say that frozen pizza is Norway's national dish, and Grandiosa is by far the most popular brand.

Given that Norway is a highly industrialized country, it's only natural that globalization has influenced its eating habits. Of course, a person can find McDonald's or Burger King in the cities, though the prices are expensive. Hot dogs are a popular lunch choice. Fine dining has also undergone a quiet culinary revolution, with top Norwegian chefs reimaging a national cuisine based on heritage and local ingredients, but which is anything but the same old boiled fish and potatoes. In 2016, for the first time ever, the esteemed Michelin Guide awarded a Norwegian restaurant, Maaemo, its top rating of three out of three stars.

Nevertheless, Norway's traditional cuisine has much to recommend it. Living close to the sea, Norwegians have historically depended on seafood for much of their diet. Cooks prepare fish in various ways, frequently serving it with boiled potatoes and vegetables during the main meal of the day, *middag* (mid-DAHG), which usually takes place

Norwegian cuisine may not be as internationally popular as French, Italian, or Chinese, but the Norwegian population is one of the healthiest in the world, according to the Norwegian Institute of Public Health, and diet has a great deal to do with it.

Open-face sandwiches of herring fillets, onions, pickles, and dill on brown bread are traditional meals in Norway.

between 4 and 6 p.m. Norwegians typically eat three other meals—breakfast, lunch, and supper. Each meal features *smørbrød* (SMUHR-brur), open-faced sandwiches of bread or crackers layered with cheese, jam, salmon spread, boiled egg, tomato, cucumber, sausage, herring, or sardines.

Some Norwegian delicacies are salty and have a strong odor. *Gravet* (grah-VUHT), or smoked salmon, is a favorite, and some Norwegians savor *rakørret* (RAHK-uhr-ruht), or trout aged for months until it has a soft, buttery consistency and a pungent odor. Lamb is the most common meat, and blood sausage—a mixture of blood and flour—is a national specialty.

Traditional desserts include fruit soups, *rømmegrøt* (RUH-muh-gruhrt), or sour cream porridge, and fresh berries during the summer.

SMØRGÅSBORD

Smørgåsbord (SMUHR-gaws-boor), a word that has entered the English vocabulary as "smorgasbord" means an overflowing buffet table and an opportunity to indulge oneself. Smørgåsbord is a Swedish word to describe the Scandinavian practice of laying out a buffet spread with a multitude of different dishes, from spicy cured herring and other fish to meats, salads, and cheeses. The term literally means "bread and butter table," and the idea is that one helps oneself to various dishes and eats them with bread and butter. The actual Norwegian (and Danish) name is *koldtbord* (KOLT-boor), which means cold table, but the Swedish word is better known and generally used. A ritual is attached to the smorgasbord. One must begin with the various cured herring,

A smorgasbord of seafood choices is offered at a restaurant in Kristiansand.

take a fresh plate for the meats and salads, and then finish up with cheese. The usual adult beverages served during a smorgasbord are schnapps, aquavit (AH-qeh-vit), and beer.

TYPICAL DISHES

Almost every Norwegian dish includes potatoes—sliced, boiled, fried, in stews, and in any other way imaginable. The potato has been a staple of the Norwegian diet since the early nineteenth century.

Norwegians eat a heavily meat- and fish-based diet. A children's favorite is *kjøttkaker* (shet-KAH-ker), or meatballs in brown sauce. Norwegians have been known to take canned kjøttkaker with them when traveling in case they do not get accustomed to the local food. *Fårikål* (fawr-EE-kawl) is a traditional thick, rich lamb stew cooked with cabbage. This is often made in the fall when lamb is abundant. *Fiskeboller* (fis-kuh-BOWL-er), or Norwegian fishballs made from a mixture of fish, salt, and water, are an acquired taste. *Lapskaus* (lahps-KAH-oos), a meat and potato stew made with salted pork or leftover meats, is a thick, chunky stew popular with everyone.

Lutefisk (LEW-tuh-fisk), usually served a few weeks before Christmas, is most definitely an acquired taste. It is prepared by soaking dried cod in lye water for two or three days until the flesh is soft enough to poke a finger through. The cod is then soaked in running cold water for two days to

Holiday *lefse* is rolled on a plate.

remove all traces of lye, and then cut into large pieces and boiled or poached. Lutefisk is often served with *lefse* (LEHF-suh), or Norwegian flatbread, and can be eaten with peas or white sauce and mustard.

"Finnish beef" is not really beef at all, but a Sami speciality made from very thin slices of reindeer meat browned in butter and seasoned with salt and pepper. It is often served with some goat cheese, lingonberry jelly, and, of course, boiled or mashed potatoes.

MUSHROOM AND BERRY PICKING

More Norwegians are acquiring a taste for mushrooms. This increasing interest has developed into a pastime of nature walks combined with mushroom picking. Berry picking, on the other hand, has long been a leisure activity for the entire family. The rewards of both mushroom and berry picking include delicious dishes, jams, and pies.

Norway's vast forests are public domain, even if parts of them are owned by farmers. There is a right of public access to all forested areas in Norway, and everyone is free to pick mushrooms or berries.

In late summer there are lush bushes full of wild raspberries just waiting to be made into scrumptious desserts. In the fall the mountains are bursting with other luscious berries, including blueberries, lingonberries (a tart, cranberry-like berry very popular in Norway and often made into jelly), and the less abundant, tart cloudberries, a Scandinavian delicacy.

CHEESE, ANYONE?

Norwegian cheeses include Gulost, Gamalost, and Pultost. The famous brands are Jarlsberg, Gudbrandsdal, and Ridder. Jarlsberg, popular in Norway, is also the best known outside of the country. Gudbrandsdal is cheese that

From hot chocolate to candy bars, chocolate is a Norwegian passion. Every Norwegian consumes, on average, 17.6 pounds (8 kilograms) of chocolate a year. Half of this is produced by Freia.

Freia is Norway's most famous chocolate factory, immortalized in Roald Dahl's enormously popular book (and movie) Charlie and the Chocolate Factory. Freia had its beginnings in 1892 when founder Johan Throne Holst, with his brother and brother-in-law, bought a small chocolate factory in the Rødeløkka district in Oslo. Freia, which is still located in Rødeløkka, is one of Norway's great success stories. One of every two chocolate bars sold in Norway is made by Freia, and the company also exports chocolates all over the world. Its motto is "A little piece of Norway."

Over the years, the company has contributed more than just chocolate to Norwegian society. Freia gained an early endorsement by famous Norwegian explorer Roald Amundsen. After his return from his 1911 South Pole expedition, he said that Freia chocolate was one of his team's main sources of nourishment during the grueling journey.

In 1920, Freia created Freia Park, one of Oslo's finest parks, exhibiting the works of European sculptors, including Norwegian Gustav Vigeland. In 1922, Freia invited Norwegian artist Edvard Munch to decorate its employees' lunchroom. The company still exhibits those paintings today. And, in 1934, Freia Hall, home of the Oslo Philharmonic Orchestra, was opened.

Today the company is owned by Mondelez International, the former Kraft Foods Inc. Tours of the chocolate factory, called Freialand, is a favorite activity for school groups and tourists.

is regarded as the most Norwegian. First made in the 1850s in Fron in the Gudbrandsdalen area, this red cheese is most popular at the Norwegian breakfast table due to its sweet, caramelized flavor. Gamalost means old cheese, and this sharp-flavored cheese is well named, both for its pungent odor and because it has roots going back to Viking times.

BEER AND WINE

Beer drinking is a Scandinavian tradition. During Viking times and the Middle Ages, beer was served at formal occasions. Whether it is to make an agreement legally binding or to celebrate the baptism of an infant or a wedding, beer is served. As the price of beer is high in Norway, many Norwegians brew their own beer in the basements of their homes.

Wine is also popular, but as Norway's climate is unsuitable for grape cultivation, Norwegians make wine from other fruits and from flowers. Wine making is a popular hobby. Fruit and flower wines must be aged for a year but, with their refreshing taste, they are well worth the wait.

COFFEE

Traders brought coffee to Norway about 250 years ago, but as it was both foreign and expensive, only the wealthy consumed it. Modern Norwegians have made up for lost time with a vengeance. Norwegians consume an average of 12.25 pounds (5.4 kg) per person, making them the world's biggest consumers of coffee per inhabitant. And they are coffee purists who prefer to drink their coffee black to savor its full aroma and flavor. Guests are usually served coffee with cakes or smørbrød.

AQUAVIT: THE NATIONAL DRINK

Aquavit, known as Scandinavia's cross-national drink, was first sold in the sixteenth century as a medicinal potion. Eske Bille, who created the drink in 1531, named it *Aqua Vitæ* ("water of life"), called it "a cure for all ills," and over the years this liquor graduated from medicinal potion to social beverage. Aquavit is made from potatoes and flavored with orange peel and several spices, including anise, fennel, caraway, and coriander. Aquavit is traditionally served with appetizers but it can also be served as an after-dinner drink.

The best-known aquavit in Europe is Linie Aquavit, or line aquavit, so called because the aquavit has passed over the Equator. Many years ago, ships setting out from Trøndelag carried Norwegian aquavit on board as an export product. Not all the aquavit was sold, and when sampling the remainder, people noticed that the long journey had given the aquavit a new, enticing aroma. Since 1850, aquavit has been aged in oak vats on ships plying the route between Norway and Australia. Every bottle of aquavit has the name of the ship it was aged aboard, where it has been, and the duration of the journey recorded on its label.

A bottle of Linie aquavit

INTERNET LINKS

www.freia.no
The home of Freia chocolate, this site can be translated into imperfect English, but it's still worth a visit.

www.visitnorway.com/things-to-do/taste-norway
This travel site has a particularly good section on Norwegian cuisine.

NORSK FISKEGRATENG (NORWEGIAN FISH GRATIN)

This is a typical home recipe, well loved by children and adults alike. Some versions include cooked macaroni and/or grated cheese mixed into the gratin.

1 ½ pounds (700 grams) cod, haddock, or
   other white fish fillets, poached
½ cup (75 g) frozen peas, thawed
⅓ cup butter
½ cup (60 g) white flour
2 cups milk (475 milliliters), warmed
1 teaspoon salt
Dash nutmeg
⅛ tsp pepper
3 eggs, separated
buttered bread crumbs

Flake the poached fish into a well buttered baking dish. Sprinkle in peas, if using.

Make a white sauce: In a small saucepan, melt butter, and add flour. Stir together over a low heat to make a roux. Gradually add the milk, stirring constantly with a whisk. Stir a few spoonfuls of hot milk mixture into egg yolks to temper, then whisk egg yolk mixture into the milk sauce. Beat thoroughly over medium heat until smooth and thickened. Whisk in salt, pepper, and nutmeg.

In a large bowl, beat egg whites until stiff. Gently fold sauce into the whites. Pour over the fish and top with a layer of buttered breadcrumbs.

Bake at 350°F (175°C) for 30—45 minutes. Serve with melted butter, boiled potatoes, and grated carrot salad (such as raw grated carrot tossed with orange juice).

FYRSTEKAKE (ROYALTY CAKE OR ALMOND TART)

Crust:
1¼ cups (150 g) all-purpose flour
1 teaspoon baking powder
½ tsp salt
½ cup (1 stick) (120 g) unsalted butter
½ cup (100 g) sugar
1 large egg yolk
2 tsp whole milk or heavy cream
Filling:
2 cups (300 g) slivered almonds
1 cup (50 g) powdered sugar
½ tsp each ground cardamom, cinnamon, and/or nutmeg (opt)
3 large egg whites
½ tsp vanilla extract
1 large egg yolk, beaten with 2 tsp water

Combine flour, sugar, baking powder, butter, and seasonings in a food processor until crumbly. Add the egg yolk and milk and continue to process just until the dough comes together. Form the dough into a disk and cover with plastic wrap. Refrigerate for at least two hours.

Butter a 9-inch (23-centimeter) tart pan with a removable bottom. Break off about one quarter of dough and set aside. Scatter small pieces of remaining dough over bottom of tart pan. Using fingertips, press dough onto bottom and up sides of pan. Roll out smaller dough piece to about ⅛-inch (1.27 cm) thick. Cut into ½-inch strips or, alternatively, decorative shapes using cookie cutters. Place on a parchment paper-lined baking sheet. Cover and chill cutouts while you prepare filling.

Preheat oven to 350°F (175°C). Pulse almonds, powdered sugar, and spices in a food processor until nuts are finely ground. Transfer dry ingredients to a large bowl. Using an electric mixer, beat egg whites and vanilla in a medium bowl until medium peaks form. Gently fold egg whites into dry ingredients.

Fill chilled crust with almond mixture; smooth top. Arrange strips into lattice or arrange cutouts on top and brush top with egg wash. Bake tart until golden brown and filling is set, 30—35 minutes. Transfer to a wire rack; let cool. Serves 8—12.

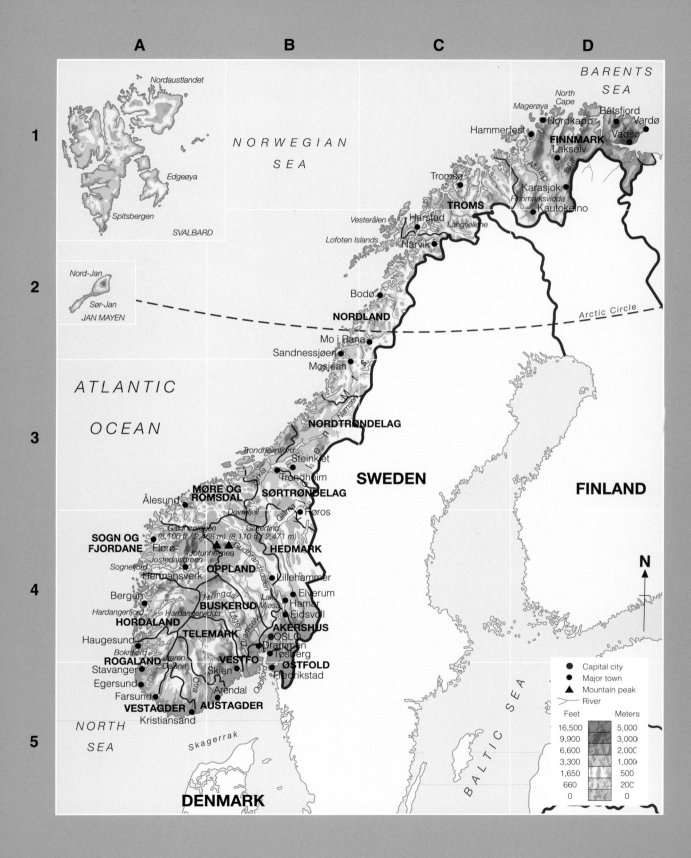

A   **B**   **C**   **D**

1

Nordaustlandet

*BARENTS
SEA*

Magerøya   *North
Cape*

Hammerfest   Nordkapp   Bätsfjord   Vardø

FINNMARK   Vadsø

Lakselv

*NORWEGIAN
SEA*

Edgeøya

Tromsø

Spitsbergen

Karasjok

Finnmarksvidda

Kautokeino

SVALBARD

TROMS

Vesterålen   Harstad   *Langfjellene*

Lofoten Islands   Narvik

2

Nord-Jan

Sør-Jan

JAN MAYEN

Bodø

Arctic Circle

NORDLAND

Mo i Rana

ATLANTIC

Sandnessjøen

Mosjøen

3

OCEAN

Namsen

NORDTRØNDELAG

Trondheimfjord

Steinkjet

Trondheim

SWEDEN

FINLAND

Orkla   *Glama*   Røros

**MØRE OG
ROMSDAL**

SØRTRØNDELAG

Ålesund

Dovrefjell

Galdhøpiggen   *Glittertind*

(8,100 ft / 2,468 m)   (8,110 ft / 2,471 m)

**SOGN OG
FJORDANE**   Florø

Jotunheimen

HEDMARK

Jostedalsbreen

OPPLAND

Sognefjord   Hermansverk

N

4

Bergen

Lillehammer

BUSKERUD

Hallingdal

Elverum

*Lake
Mjøsa*   Hamar

Hardangerfjord   *Hardangervidda*

Eidsvoll

HORDALAND

TELEMARK

AKERSHUS

Haugesund

Drammer   **OSLO**

Bokritjord   Drammen

ROGALAND   *Jæren*   **VESTFO**   Tønsberg   **ØSTFOLD**

Stavanger   *Dalane*   Skien   Fredrikstad

Egersund

Arendal

Farsund

VESTAGDER   **AUSTAGDER**

NORTH

Kristiansand

5

SEA

Skagerrak

*BALTIC
SEA*

● Capital city
● Major town
▲ Mountain peak
〜 River

Feet	Meters
16,500	5,000
9,900	3,000
6,600	2,000
3,300	1,000
1,650	500
660	200
0	0

DENMARK

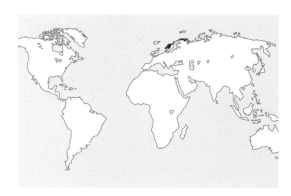

ECONOMIC NORWAY

Agriculture

- Barley
- Beef
- Milk
- Pork
- Potatoes
- Wheat

Manufacturing

- **Al** Aluminum
- Chemicals
- Fish processing
- Paper

Natural Resources

- Copper
- Hydropower
- Iron
- Timber

Services

- Airport
- Port
- Tourism
- Train station

ABOUT THE ECONOMY

POPULATION
5.2 million (2015)

GROSS DOMESTIC PRODUCT
$397.6 billion (2015)

GDP GROWTH
0.9 percent (2015)

INFLATION RATE
2.0 percent (2015)

CURRENCY
1 Norwegian krone (NOK) = 100 øre
Notes: 50, 100, 200, 500, 1,000 kroner
Coins: 50 øre, 1 krone, and 5, 10, and
20 kroner
1 USD = 8.32 NOK (April 2016)

NATURAL RESOURCES
Petroleum, natural gas, iron ore, copper,
lead, zinc, titanium, pyrites, nickel, fish,
timber, hydropower

AGRICULTURAL PRODUCTS
Barley, wheat, potatoes; pork, beef, veal,
milk; fish

INDUSTRIES
Petroleum and gas, shipping, fishing,
aquaculture, food processing, shipbuilding,
pulp and paper products, metals,
chemicals, timber, mining, textiles

MAJOR EXPORTS
Petroleum and petroleum products,
machinery and equipment, metals,
chemicals, ships, fish

MAJOR IMPORTS
Machinery and equipment, chemicals,
metals, foodstuffs

MAIN TRADE PARTNERS
Sweden, Germany, France, Denmark,
United Kingdom, Netherlands, United
States, China, Japan

LABOR FORCE
2 8 million (2015)

UNEMPLOYMENT RATE
4.4 percent (2015)

AIRPORTS
95; 67 with paved runways; 28 unpaved
(2013)

INTERNET USERS
4.9 million, 96.2 percent of population
(2014)

CULTURAL NORWAY

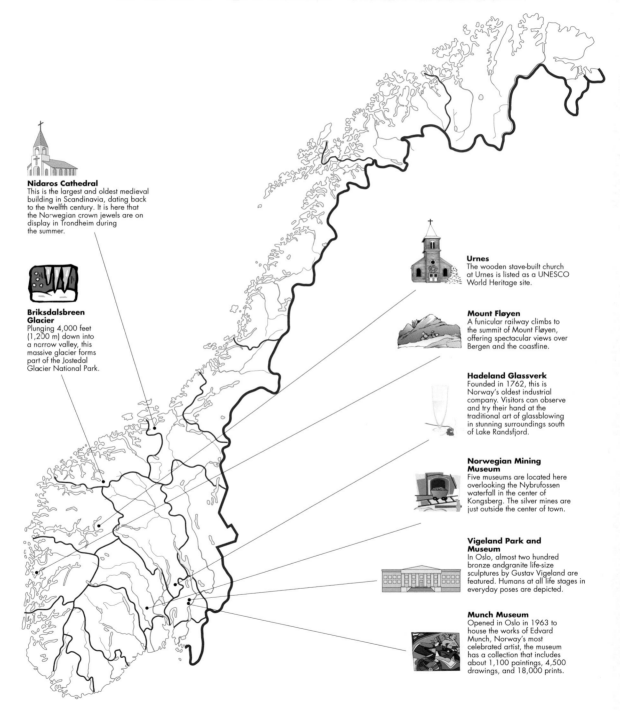

Nidaros Cathedral
This is the largest and oldest medieval building in Scandinavia, dating back to the twelfth century. It is here that the Norwegian crown jewels are on display in Trondheim during the summer.

Briksdalsbreen Glacier
Plunging 4,000 feet (1,200 m) down into a narrow valley, this massive glacier forms part of the Jostedal Glacier National Park.

Urnes
The wooden stave-built church at Urnes is listed as a UNESCO World Heritage site.

Mount Fløyen
A funicular railway climbs to the summit of Mount Fløyen, offering spectacular views over Bergen and the coastline.

Hadeland Glassverk
Founded in 1762, this is Norway's oldest industrial company. Visitors can observe and try their hand at the traditional art of glassblowing in stunning surroundings south of Lake Randsfjord.

Norwegian Mining Museum
Five museums are located here overlooking the Nybrufossen waterfall in the center of Kongsberg. The silver mines are just outside the center of town.

Vigeland Park and Museum
In Oslo, almost two hundred bronze and granite life-size sculptures by Gustav Vigeland are featured. Humans at all life stages in everyday poses are depicted.

Munch Museum
Opened in Oslo in 1963 to house the works of Edvard Munch, Norway's most celebrated artist, the museum has a collection that includes about 1,100 paintings, 4,500 drawings, and 18,000 prints.

ABOUT THE CULTURE

OFFICIAL NAME
Kingdom of Norway, Kongeriket Norge (in Norwegian)

CAPITAL
Oslo

NATIONAL FLAG
Red with a blue cross outlined in white that extends to the edges of the flag; the vertical part of the cross is shifted to the hoist side.

TOTAL AREA
Approximately 150,000 square miles (388,850 sq km), including the island territories of Svalbard and Jan Mayen.

ETHNIC GROUPS
Norwegian 94.4 percent (includes Sami, about 60,000); other European 3.6 percent; other, 2.0 percent (2007)

RELIGIOUS GROUPS
Lutheran Church of Norway 82.1 percent; other Christian 3.9 percent; Islam 2.3 percent; Roman Catholic 1.8 percent; other, 2.4; unspecified 7.5 percent (2011)

MAIN LANGUAGES
Norwegian (Bokmål and Nynorsk)

LITERACY
100 percent

LIFE EXPECTANCY AT BIRTH
Total: 81.7 years
Male: 79.7 years
Female: 83.8 years (2015)

ROYAL FAMILY
Harald V, King of Norway (b. 1937), ascended the throne January 17, 1991, succeeding his father, King Olav V.
Sonja, Queen of Norway (b. 1937)
Haakon Magnus, Crown Prince of Norway (b. 1973)
Märtha Louise, Princess of Norway (b. 1971)

TIMELINE

IN NORWAY	IN THE WORLD
10,000 BCE First human settlers reach Norway.	**753 BCE** Rome is founded.
	116–117 CE The Roman Empire reaches its greatest extent.
	600 Height of Mayan civilization
770 CE Viking Age begins.	
900 Norway is united into one kingdom.	
995 Christianity is introduced into Norway.	
1217 Haakon IV becomes king.	**1000** The Chinese perfect gunpowder and begin to use it in warfare.
1349 The Black Death kills two-thirds of the population.	
1450 Norway becomes part of Denmark.	
	1530 Beginning of transatlantic slave trade.
	1620 Pilgrims sail the *Mayflower* to America.
	1776 US Declaration of Independence
1814 Union with Denmark ends. New union with Sweden begins.	**1789–1799** The French Revolution
	1861 The US Civil War begins.
1884 Parliamentary system is established.	**1869** The Suez Canal is opened.
1905 Sweden recognizes independent Kingdom of Norway. Danish Prince Carl is elected king.	
1913 Norwegian women gain the right to vote.	**1914** World War I begins.
	1939 World War II begins.

IN NORWAY	IN THE WORLD
1940	
Norway is invaded and occupied by Germany. Prime Minister Johan Nygaardsvold leads the government in exile (1940–1945).	
1945	**1945**
Norway joins the United Nations.	World War II ends.
1949	**1949**
Norway becomes a member of NATO.	The North Atlantic Treaty Organization (NATO) is formed.
	1957
	The Russians launch *Sputnik 1*.
	1966–1969
1968	The Chinese Cultural Revolution
Norway discovers oil in the North Sea.	
1972	
Norwegians vote not to join the European Union.	
1981	
Norway elects first female prime minister.	**1986**
	Nuclear power disaster at Chernobyl in Ukraine
1991	**1991**
King Olav V dies; King Harald V ascends the throne.	Breakup of the Soviet Union
1993	
Norway resumes commercial whaling despite international moratorium.	
1994	
Second vote against joining the European Union.	**1997**
	Hong Kong is returned to China.
2001–2005	**2001**
Norway is ranked top in UN Human Development Index.	Terrorists attack the US on 9/11.
2007	**2003**
Constitution amended to abolish bicameral division of Storting parliament.	War in Iraq
	2008
	US elects first African-American president, Barack Obama.
2015	**2016**
Five thousand refugees from Syria, Iraq, and Afghanistan cross into Norway from Russia.	Islamist terrorists attack Belgium.

GLOSSARY

ætt (eht)
Group of eight letters in the twenty-four-rune alphabet.

allmannsretten (AWL-leh-mawns-reht-ten)
Every man's right to public access of the countryside.

barnehage (BAR-neh-HAH-guh)
Kindergarten for children ages four to seven.

Bokmål (BOOK-mawl)
Language developed during Norway's union with Denmark. The spoken form is different from Danish, but the written form is nearly identical to Danish.

bunad (BOO-nahd)
Embroidered national dress.

fjord (fyord)
Very deep and narrow inlet of the sea between steep cliffs.

futhark (FEW-thark)
A name for the runic alphabet created by the first six letters of the alphabet.

fylker (FEWL-ker)
Counties.

husmorlag (HEWS-moor-lahg)
Neighborhood group of women who do projects of common interest

joik (yoy-IK)
Sami musical tradition of yodeling that imitates animal sounds.

kommuner (koo-MEW-ner)
Rural or urban district belonging to a county; each is administered by a council.

kvinnegruppe (KVIN-nuh-GREW-puh)
Women's group formed to discuss women's issues and contemporary literature.

middag (mid-DAHG)
Main meal of the day, eaten around 4 to 6 p.m.

Nynorsk (NEE-noshk)
Language created in reaction to Danish rule, dating from the mid-1800s and combining elements from rural dialects for a more distinctly Norwegian language than Bokmål.

runes (roons)
Angular letters of an ancient alphabet, one of the earliest forms of Germanic writing.

russ (rewss)
High-school graduates celebrate their graduation wearing russ gowns.

Samnorsk (SAHM-noshk)
"Common Norwegian," a language created by twentieth century language experts who sought to streamline Bokmål and Nynorsk into one language.

Storting (stoor-TING)
Norway's 169-member parliament.

vidder (VI-der)
Mountain plateaus.

FOR FURTHER INFORMATION

BOOKS

Booth, Michael. *The Almost Nearly Perfect People: Behind the Myth of the Scandinavian Utopia.* New York: Picador, 2014.

Braun, Eric. *Norway in Pictures.* Minneapolis, MN: Lerner Publications, 2003.

DK Eyewitness Travel Guide: Norway. New York: DK Publishing, revised 2014.

Gallagher, Thomas. *Assault in Norway: Sabotaging The Nazi Nuclear Program.* Guilford, CT: Globe Pequot Press, reissued 2010.

Seierstad, Anna. *One of Us: The Story of a Massacre in Norway—And Its Aftermath.* New York: Farrar, Strauss and Giroux, 2013.

WEBSITES

BBC News. Norway country profile. www.bbc.com/news/world-europe-17743896

CIA World Factbook. Norway. www.cia.gov/library/publications/the-world-factbook/geos/no.html

Government.no. www.regjeringen.no/en/id4

Lonely Planet. www.lonelyplanet.com/norway

Stortinget. www.stortinget.no/en/In-English

VisitNorway.com. www.visitnorway.com

FILMS

Norway: From the Land of Vikings. Trailwood Films & Media, 2010.

MUSIC

Folk Music from Norway. Norway Music, 1996.

Grieg: Peer Gynt Suites, Holberg Suite, Berlin Philharmonic Orchestra, Deutsche Grammophon, 1993

Nordisk Sang, New Albion Records, 2009.

Norwegian Classical Favourites, Iceland Symphony Orchestra. Naxos, 2004.

White Night: Impressions of Norwegian Folk Music, BIS, 2011.

BIBLIOGRAPHY

BBC News. Norway country profile. http://www.bbc.com/news/world-europe-17743896.

CIA World Factbook. Norway. https://www.cia.gov/library/publications/the-world-factbook/geos/no.html.

Eurostat. Energy production and imports. http://ec.europa.eu/eurostat/statistics-explained/index.php/Energy_production_and_imports.

Kahn, Jennifer. "Healthy Habits in Norway." *Women's Health*, May 9, 2009.

Knausgaard, Karl Ove. "The Inexplicable." *The New Yorker*, May 25, 2015. http://www.newyorker.com/magazine/2015/05/25/the-inexplicable.

Lidz, Franz. "Kon-Tiki Sails Again." *The Smithsonian Magazine*, April 2013. http://www.smithsonianmag.com/history/kon-tiki-sails-again-5404357.

The Nordic Page. http://www.tnp.no.

Norway Today. http://norwaytoday.info.

Statistics Norway. https://www.ssb.no/en.

Stortinget. https://www.stortinget.no/en/In-English.

United Nations Regional Information Centre for Western Europe (Unric). "The Sami of Northern Europe—one people, four countries." http://www.unric.org/en/indigenous-people/27307-the-sami-of-northern-europe--one-people-four-countries.

WDC. Whaling in Norway. http://us.whales.org/issues/whaling-in-norway.

Williams, Thomas D. "For First Time in History, Atheism Overtakes Religious Faith in Norway." Breitbart, March 22, 2016.

INDEX

INDEX